"'Waiting on the Lord' can sound like an irritating pause-button on life until it gets back to being more exciting. But in this remarkable new book, Wayne Stiles debunks that myth, sharing how active and engaging waiting on God can be—just a few chapters, and you'll be convinced!"

—**Joni Eareckson Tada**, Joni and Friends International Disability Center

"Wayne Stiles gives a down-to-earth approach to why God puts us through periods of waiting. During that time, we learn more about trust, tolerance, faith, and sovereignty—and in the learning, we grow up. Wayne has chosen the biblical life of Joseph to teach us what God is doing—and why! And in the reading, we get a clear picture of the value of putting confidence in God rather than putting hope in our preferred plan."

—**Luci Swindoll**, author/speaker

"The seeming silence of God is a serious problem for the suffering. The life of Joseph as exposed by Wayne Stiles will be a great encouragement to anyone who has had to wait to experience God's answers. Wayne is intensely biblical and insightfully practical. He does his homework and he writes from the heart."

—**Dr. Mark L. Bailey**, president of Dallas Theological Seminary

"The story of Joseph has always captured me, but I've never filtered it through the discipline of waiting. Wayne Stiles unpacks important and practical biblical truths that will help people finally embrace patient waiting as a lifestyle."

—**Mary DeMuth**, coauthor of *The Day I Met Jesus*

"I hate to wait . . . and I'm not alone! We all want immediate answers, rapid-fire results, and instant fulfillment. But God operates on a different timetable. So how do we sync our watches with his?

Wayne Stiles shares the answer in his fascinating study on the life of Joseph. You will learn much about Joseph. But more importantly, you will learn lessons about waiting on God that will help you develop a persistent, long-term faith."

—**Dr. Charlie Dyer**, professor-at-large of Bible, Moody Bible Institute; host of *The Land and the Book* radio program

"In life, we all encounter the 'best of times and the worst of times.' My worse times are when I'm forced to wait—on a phone call, a stoplight, an important diagnosis, a long-awaited trip, you name it. Impatience is a taskmaster. And waiting on God? Well, that can be the most difficult wait of all. I gravitate to those people who help me learn how to wait with patience and perspective. Wayne Stiles is that kind of person, and his new book, *Waiting on God: What to Do When God Does Nothing*, is that kind of book. I was hooked when I read the title, and reading the book gave me insight, perspective, and even a little more patience when it comes to waiting on God. I recommend it highly. It's well written, encouraging, and for many of us, even life-changing."

—**Mary Graham**, former president of Women of Faith

WAITING
on GOD

WAITING
on GOD

What to Do When God Does Nothing

WAYNE STILES

BakerBooks

a division of Baker Publishing Group
Grand Rapids, Michigan

Published by Baker Books
a division of Baker Publishing Group
P.O. Box 6287, Grand Rapids, MI 49516-6287
www.bakerbooks.com

Printed in the United States of America

Library of Congress Cataloging-in-Publication Data
Stiles, Wayne.
    Waiting on God : what to do when God does nothing / Wayne Stiles.
      pages cm
    Includes bibliographical references.
    ISBN 978-0-8010-1845-9 (pbk. : alk. paper)
    1. Joseph (Son of Jacob) 2. Waiting (Philosophy) 3. Providence and government of God—Christianity. 4. Trust in God—Christianity. I. Title.
    BS580.J6S755 2015
    241'.4—dc23   2015009269

Published in association with MacGregor Literary, Inc.

15 16 17 18 19 20 21   7 6 5 4 3 2 1

For MATT *and* COURTNEY
And for OUR MOTHER—*who waits no longer*

CONTENTS

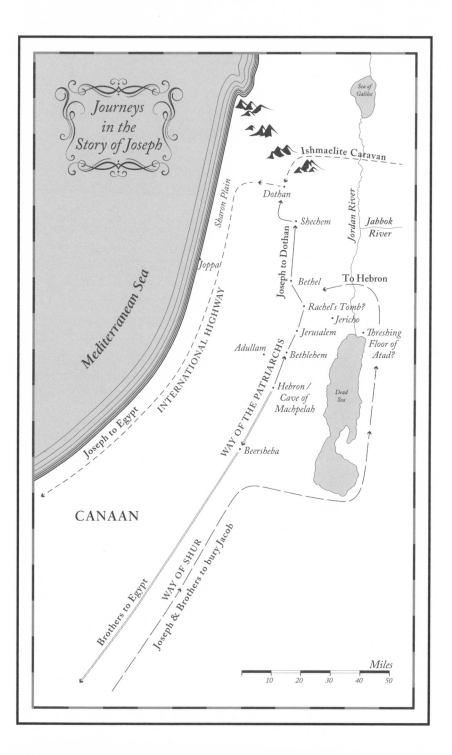

Journeys in the Story of Joseph

Sea of Galilee

Ishmaelite Caravan

Sharon Plain

Dothan

Joppa!

Shechem

Jordan River

Jabbok River

Joseph to Dothan

Bethel

To Hebron

Rachel's Tomb?

Jericho

INTERNATIONAL HIGHWAY

Mediterranean Sea

Jerusalem

Threshing Floor of Atad?

Adullam

WAY OF THE PATRIARCHS

Bethlehem

Joseph to Egypt

Hebron / Cave of Machpelah

Dead Sea

Beersheba

CANAAN

Brothers to Egypt

WAY OF SHUR

Joseph & Brothers to bury Jacob

Miles

10   20   30   40   50

He sent a man before them, Joseph, who was sold as a slave. . . . Until the time that his word came to pass, the word of the LORD tested him.

Psalm 105:17, 19

INTRODUCTION

A few years ago, my jaw dropped as I added up how much I had spent that year on highway tolls. This surprising revelation forced me to reexamine my early morning commute. I decided to take the access road to work each morning instead of the highway.

But I discovered I pay either way. I pay in time or in money. In angst or in cash. Because I seem to have more of time, I pay it at stoplights.

The worst is when the stale green light turns yellow and then stops me—with no one coming the other way. Almost as if the technicians who installed the street sensors cross-wired the lights so that the stoplight would change to red only when I approached. "Here comes Wayne; let's make him wait!" As I sit at the empty intersection, I observe all these cameras and sensors with enough technology to ticket me when I run the light but not enough know-how to help me through the intersection in a timely manner.

Five in the morning. Pitch black outside. No crosstraffic. The light turns red.

So I stop. I have stopped just to stop. Dead silent. No one around. It's just me and this long red light—plus seven cameras pointing my direction, daring me to cross the line. I imagine some officer somewhere observing me through the camera, giggling at the poor guy stopped at the light just to stop.

But there has to be a reason, I reason. *Maybe I'm stopped at this light because on the other side of town somewhere a light is green and someone else is cruising through. Maybe my light is red so that their light can be green.* I have to believe there is a reason for the red light. A *good* reason, that is.

Because I trust God, I have to believe that waiting at the light in the dark with no other traffic serves a purpose. I can see no reason to wait—except for this light. So I wait.

As I sit there morning after morning (saving money, remember), I have time to think. Lots of time.

I began to make a mental note of all the reasons we wait: stoplights, waiting rooms, suppertime, difficult meetings, paydays, slowpokes in the fast lane, slowpokes in the slow lane, anticipating meeting someone we admire, a child's athletic practice, a person who needs to change but who stays blind to their fault, weekends, inspiration to write, that first kiss, those lab results, just the right moment to have a hard conversation, someone to take a breath so others can join the conversation, tax refunds, gardens to grow, investments to grow, Christmas morning, the mail, delayed airplanes, fast food, and public restroom lines. The list ends only when life does. We do a lot of waiting.

But the most difficult kind of waiting? *Waiting on God.*

Waiting on God usually means hanging on until he changes our circumstances—be they relational, financial, physical, or even spiritual. The trouble is, God seldom seems in a hurry.

At all.

What.

So.

Ever.

Instead, God often allows our circumstances to stay the same—or even to worsen—while he waits on *us* to change.

So . . . both God and we are in a waiting game, idling in neutral until someone moves first. We want God to change situations. God wants us to change in them. We want relief. God wants repentance. We want happiness. God wants holiness. We want pleasure. God wants piety. It's like a game of Ping-Pong. Or tug-of-war.

God always wins in this game.

It feels like we're kids again, playing "Red Light Green Light"— but this time with the Almighty. As soon as we start to inch forward, God spins around and shouts, "Red light!"

Most of the time, all we can clearly see are the systems in place to catch us running that red light. We see very few signals that indicate God is helping us move forward.

What's more, our efforts to attempt to speed up the process of waiting, or to sidestep it, can backfire on us. Like when eggs explode in the microwave—or oatmeal glops out of the bowl, leaving nothing to eat (I never understood why that happens). We can't microwave God's plans for us.

In the end, if we really knew the big picture, we too would want what God wants for us—and in the exact way and timing he wants it to occur. It's just that our pain often blinds us to that perspective. We see only the red light. God sees the purpose—his good and loving purpose—for the delay.

And although we cannot understand why the light is there, we do know what the red light means.

Wait.

For now, that's all we need to understand.

If God determines we're going to wait, believe me, we will. We will not hurry God. The waiting is a given. But *how* will we wait? Since we're going to wait anyway, we might as well wait well. Patience, then, is the art of waiting well.

The familiarity of the verse too often camouflages its comfort: "And we know that God causes all things to work together for good to those who love God, to those who are called according to His purpose" (Rom. 8:28). Although the theology of this verse gives us the end goal, it's the getting there that bothers us. Seldom do we see what good could possibly rise from the ashes of pain we experience. We may "know" that it's true, but how does that knowledge help us in the real world of pain? What do we do when it seems God is doing nothing?

Enter Joseph.

The story of Joseph reveals, better than most, how to wait on God. But while Joseph shows us how, it's important to remember that the theme of his story in Genesis is not waiting on God. Rather, it is God's providence—his sovereign direction in our lives.

Generally speaking, God's providence in Genesis reveals his good purposes when other events—even evil ones—seem to threaten them. To get really specific, Joseph's life shows how God preserved the line of Judah—the tribe through whom the head-crushing, serpent-slaying, seed-of-woman Messiah would come. (More about that later.)

So God is sovereign. That's great. Super. But so what? That's *his* attribute, not ours. We don't have the luxury of eternity just yet. We're stuck in time and space, with all their limitations and failings. How do we apply God's sovereignty to Monday mornings?

The application of sovereignty shows itself in the life of a believer in a number of ways. It requires more than just pondering it. It even means more than worshiping God for his control (though that's a great start). I'm convinced the primary way we apply God's providence to our lives is by waiting.

We apply sovereignty by waiting on God.

Because the results of God's sovereignty are delayed, waiting remains an act of faith. We believe results will occur one day. By waiting on God, we affirm our belief in his providence. We trust his timetable. We hope in heaven. Waiting on God is inseparably bound to our belief in the sovereignty of God to bring about the good he promises.

So although Joseph's story on a theological level declares God's control and providence in our lives, on a practical level those grand truths are lived out in the trenches in time. Lots of time. That's where waiting comes in.

Waiting is often the application of many other, more abstract, biblical qualities of character. Hope, for instance, requires waiting. Faith is all about waiting. Patience and waiting are yoked together. Trust requires delayed gratification. In fact, run down your mental list of the fruit of the Spirit and see if waiting doesn't play into every single one of them (see Gal. 5:22–23).

As we journey through the life of Joseph in the chapters that follow, we will discover God is indeed working in our lives to accomplish his good purpose, even though we can't see how. We will learn to say, as Joseph did, "You meant evil against me, but God meant it for good" (Gen. 50:20). That's God's providence at work. It's his sovereignty on display. But it took years of waiting to come to pass.

One reason most people love Joseph's life—aside from the fact that it's just a great story—stems from the fact that Joseph's life is a lot like ours. We see ourselves in his life. True, we do not live in nineteenth-century-BC Egypt, but we all have had to wait on God without much clarification as to why. We've all faced the disillusionment of failed expectations. We've struggled with temptation. We've had lousy families. We've felt like God had us on a shelf. We've had close relationships we thought were lifelong crumble. We've borne the weight of circumstances so crushing nothing but time and God's mercy could mend them. Joseph's life will show us how waiting on God relates to all of these.

God revealed his plan for Joseph's future, but the Lord didn't reveal how his will would come about. Joseph's confidence had to be in God, not in God's plan. So it is with us.

We want God's plan so we can trust the plan. God hides the plan so we will trust him. So we will wait on him.

Joseph shows us how.

Part I

LEAVING HOME

1

LIVING IN THE GAPS WITH GOD

There are also many other things . . . which if they were
written in detail, I suppose that even the world itself would
not contain the books that would be written.

John 21:25

The Bible doesn't tell us everything. Not even close.

Oh sure, it tells us all we *need* to know. But it leaves out most of the details that scratch curiosity's itches. What did Jesus look like? Was Nehemiah bowlegged? Did Martha have a hysterical laugh? Was King David better looking than Brad Pitt? We'll never know.

That's because when we read the Scriptures, we see selected events. Even in the cases of individuals whose births and deaths are recorded—like Samuel or Samson or even Jesus—we read only of certain incidents. The Bible never shows the entire life of anybody.

Think about when someone asks you your own life story. What do you tell? No one has the time—and honestly, no one cares—to hear all the details from your junior high school experience. When asked, you give just the highlights. Most likely that's all you remember anyway.

Occasionally, though, we encounter individuals who do remember the details. *All* of them. They'll drivel on about the color of the tablecloth, or how Uncle Bob is related to Holly's cousin, or the date and time Junior lost his tooth, etcetera, etcetera, and so on. During these insufferable eternities of benevolent listening, we find ourselves squirming in our seats, counting the floor tiles, hoping our cell phone would ring, or praying for the rapture.

Because time and especially patience are limited, most people really appreciate the bottom line. Frankly, I'm grateful the Bible gives it.

With too many details, we'd get lost in the weeds. We would see so much truth that we'd understand little of it. That's why the Spirit of God selected only certain events to record in the Bible. This has a practical reason as well. The apostle John wrote, "There are also many other things which Jesus did, which if they were written in detail, I suppose that even the world itself would not contain the books that would be written" (John 21:25). Practically, there just isn't space in any book—or all books—to record everything. So the author has to make decisions. It's not dishonest. It's just practical.

I have to smile at the brevity with which the Bible records Jacob and Esau's childhood. In one verse the twins are in the womb and in the next verse they are young men pursuing life. God usually records only the life-changing, pivotal events in the lives of those in Scripture.

By eliminating most events and giving us the bottom line, God exercises his prerogative to reveal what he wants us to know—to declare the nitty-gritty of his theme for a particular book or passage. The Spirit of God inspired Matthew, for example, to emphasize a different aspect of Jesus's life than Luke recorded. The same held true centuries earlier in the books of Kings and Chronicles—same historical subjects, but the books had different purposes. Go even further back, and we see Deuteronomy restating the Law to a new generation of Hebrews.

In selecting some but not all events, God wasn't trying to smooth over embarrassing episodes or spin some revisionist history. His purpose was not to hide truth but to communicate particular truths. Most events, by necessity, had to end up on the editing floor.

That can pose a problem for us. Because the biblical narratives usually reflect only the turning points, we tend to see biblical lives as nothing but nonstop action. One only has to read the book of Ruth or about the life of Paul to see God's providence very involved in their lives. It's exciting stuff!

Our lives, by comparison, seem, well—*dull*. We'll go for years without a significant event. As a result, when we read the Bible we may assume it isn't applicable, or that God is angry with us, or that he sees us as insignificant—or worse, that we aren't even saved. We'll think, *God, why aren't you working in my life like you did in biblical days?*

When we hear exceptional testimonies at church or during a conference, the words can have the opposite effect than their intent. Instead of inspiring us to worship a God who works wonders, we find ourselves wondering, *Where are all the normal people? Or if that is normal . . . what's wrong with me?*

———

We need to remember that between significant events in the Bible lay large gaps of time. Weeks, months, years, sometimes even centuries. Even though the Bible omits the gaps, they are there. We can't forget that. We mustn't.

Most of life is lived in the gaps between great moments. The peaks seem to protrude only after miles and miles of death valleys. While the Bible reveals its characters in terms of their high points, we, on the other hand, tend to evaluate our lives by the lousy week we just slogged through. We read and assess the Bible intellectually, but we evaluate our own lives emotionally. Sometimes that disconnect seems huge. And often, discouraging.

But gaps are normal. And expecting gaps is essential if we hope to maintain a life of faith as well as discern God's hand in our lives. Even Jesus's life had gaps—huge ones. We need to accept the gaps between great moments as God's will, but we also must learn how to live in these dull spaces.

Because most of life is gaps, we never know which days will prove significant. We have the obvious exceptions, of course, like births, graduations, weddings, and occasionally even deaths. But the list drops off after these few predictables. Only hindsight reveals the significant days of God's sovereign design. God sees them in advance.

Bored with these monotonous cracks that make up most of life, we try to fill them with significant experiences. We'll change hairdos. We'll change spouses. We'll take vacations. We'll set dates for the coming of Christ. Anything to avoid the humdrum sameness of life in the gaps.

But God arranges the gaps as well as the great days. The mundane days remain an essential path to the great ones. So what do we do in the gaps?

We wait on God.

We're not waiting on God for significant days. That never works. If we live for the hope of seeing significant days in life, we'll toss in the towel. The gaps are simply too long. We need a different goal: faithfulness rather than significance. Pascal wrote, "The strength of a man's virtue must not be measured by his efforts, but by his ordinary life."[1] If the Lord chooses to make a day significant, that's great. But that's his business entirely. Significant days are God's to ordain, not ours to arrange or manipulate.

It took Joseph's family a long time to learn that truth.

Even in a life that spans many chapters in the Bible, we see gaps. Joseph lived one hundred and ten years, but the Bible only focuses on his first forty-some. The majority of his life reads as a summary.

Because God selected which events of Joseph's life to record, we know God had his reasons for what we read. Part of that purpose we understand from Paul's general principle regarding the Old Testament: "Whatever was written in earlier times was written for our instruction, so that through perseverance and the encouragement of the Scriptures we might have hope" (Rom. 15:4). God selected events to give us hope while we wait.

Joseph came into the world as the firstborn of his mother, Rachel. Two phrases from her lips explain the meaning behind Joseph's name. She said, "God has *taken away* [*asap*] my reproach," and "May the LORD *give* [*yosep*] me another son" (Gen. 30:23–24, emphasis added). The Hebrew assonance between *asap* and *yosep* reveals that Joseph's name came not only from Rachel's experience but also from her hope—both firmly grounded in God. Joseph's very name reflected faith—a prayer—a hope in God to do more than he had done already. Although God would honor Rachel's request for another son, she also hoped to live to enjoy both boys. She wouldn't.

Think back to your first-grade year. Got the picture in your mind? You were about six or seven years old. Can you recall your schoolteacher? Or your best friend at that time? What was the class bully's first name? Can you draw the floor plan of the home where you lived? You probably remember more than you think—especially if any major events occurred at that time.

When I turned six my family moved across San Antonio to a different house. That meant a new school, new neighborhood, new friends, new teachers—new everything. I even had a new baby brother. To this day, when I return to those few suburban blocks, I can point to places with hundreds of memories—all permanently etched in my mind. In fact, most of what I remember begins at age six.

That's how old Joseph was when his family moved to Canaan from Paddan-Aram—a journey of about eight hundred miles (see Gen. 30:25–43; 31:41). Talk about a major move! The baby in the family, Joseph had an older sister and ten older brothers—half-siblings from one father and four mothers—all dwelling together.

Can you imagine Joseph's father, Jacob, dealing with the angst of four wives? How about Joseph's mother, Rachel, sharing her husband with three other women? Now add twelve half-siblings to the mix (and one more brother to come). The family would have made a great reality show. Or better still, a sitcom.

From our perspective, Joseph's family of origin looks more like some aberrant cult than the seedbed for the tribes of Israel. The family had dysfunction smeared all over it. Their history included marital manipulation, sibling rivalry, bitterness, and backbiting—and that was just Joseph's parents. Joseph and his siblings learned from the pros.

The father of the family, Jacob, learned how to lie from his own mother, Rebekah. God had promised that Jacob would have preeminence over his twin brother, Esau. Nevertheless, Rebekah refused to wait on God to bring about his will in his time. She modeled how to get what you want through deception and strategic maneuvering. She convinced Jacob to lie to his father, Isaac, and steal the blessing he had intended for Jacob's brother, Esau. Bad plan.

As a result of this trickery, the heel-grabber Jacob had to flee from the murderous intentions of Esau, east across the Fertile Crescent. Jacob would never see his mother again.

In Paddan-Aram, Jacob met his match in his uncle Laban. Jacob offered to work seven years for Laban in order to marry his lovely daughter Rachel. But Laban switched daughters at the last minute, tricking Jacob into working an additional seven years in order to have Rachel as well, the bride he wanted in the first place. Each of Jacob's wives brought along a maid, both of whom became his concubines, and the four of these women swayed Mr. Milquetoast with everything from manipulations to mandrakes.

In short, after twenty years of hard labor, Jacob returned to Canaan with four wives, a dozen kids, numerous flocks and herds— and some deep-seated, deceptive patterns of family behavior in tow. This was not a family that waited on God.

All of this before Joseph's sixth birthday. From ages six to seventeen—some of the most formative years for any child—Joseph's life appears only in slices. The Bible hides the gaps of his life.

Even before the family crossed the Jordan River to return into Canaan, Joseph would have detected the tension that surrounded Jacob's final words with Uncle Laban. Joseph likely asked his mother why his father sent the family across the Jabbok River and yet he stayed behind—and why the following morning Daddy limped. Joseph had never met his uncle Esau, Jacob's brother, but Jacob's jumpiness about the get-together would have been obvious to the boy. Joseph watched as Jacob sent his other three wives and their children ahead to meet Esau, putting Rachel and Joseph in the back of the line—in the place of most protection and thus in the position most prominent.

Daddy's favorite son was becoming obvious.

Joseph's many childhood experiences included moving to a new home in Shechem, seeing the pregnant bump grow under his mom's apron (Joseph's first full sibling), and hearing of the rape of his sister Dinah at Shechem and the brutal revenge taken by Simeon and Levi. Another major move occurred south toward Hebron, after which Joseph's brother Reuben had incestuous relations with his stepmother. Joseph also would have remembered the death of his granddad Isaac and his burial in the cave of Machpelah in Hebron.

But the most significant event would have been the death of his mother as she gave birth to his brother Benjamin. Try to imagine the pain and confusion in Joseph's heart when he learned that his mom's complicated delivery had resulted in her untimely death. As the family traveled south along the ridge road today called "The Way of the Patriarchs," they buried Rachel by the side of the road on the way to Bethlehem. Joseph would never forget it.

All of Joseph's brothers grew to model their parents' and grandparents' examples of deceit, manipulation, family secrets, self-interest, lying, and sibling rivalry. Joseph had a front-row seat to the relational and emotional fallout that occurred from the backwash of such a family.

All of this leads up to the fact that life was ready to hand Joseph a raw deal. Circumstances had set him up to carry the torch of dysfunction to his own children. Joseph was cut from the same cloth. The die was cast. The mold was set. Take two. Ditto.

But God had other plans for Joseph.

When Joseph's narrative begins in Genesis 37, he has grown into a strapping young man of seventeen. And in a mere four verses we see the family's dysfunction still pulsating strong. In fact, it festered into hostility by means of yet another of father Jacob's vices.

Jacob had given Joseph a position of responsibility, like a foreman, over the family's shepherding operation. But when you have rascals for brothers, what can you bring to your father but a bad report? Imagine the older brothers' irritation of having their little brother tattle on them. Especially if the bad report proved accurate.

In addition to giving Joseph responsibility, the aging father gifted him a special coat. The King James Bible calls it the "coat of many colours" (Gen. 37:3). Whether the phrase refers to a full-length robe or to a richly ornamented tunic, it had the same effect on the brothers. Joseph might as well have worn a sandwich board that read on the front, "DADDY'S FAVORITE," and on the back, "THAT MEANS MORE FAVORITE THAN YOU."

What in the world was Jacob thinking? He tossed tradition to the wind and skipped over ten older sons to bestow blessings on the firstborn of the favorite wife. How nice. That stuck in the other brothers' craws. The coat likely revealed Jacob's selection as to who would have preeminence long-term. Regardless, the brothers knew the coat meant more than their father's choice of who would be boss. To them, it also symbolized their father's love.

All parents have natural reactions to their children's behavior. As Solomon wrote, "A wise son makes a father glad, but a foolish son is a grief to his mother" (Prov. 10:1). Parental gladness or grief often depends on the child's behavior. That's basic. It's natural. And yet that wasn't the case with Joseph. Jacob's favoritism toward Joseph had more to do with Jacob than with Joseph. The boy was his father's son in his old age, the firstborn from his favorite wife. It was all about Jacob clinging to a memory of a dream that he had buried on the way to Bethlehem.

Just as Jacob had done with the family lineup before meeting Esau, so he continued to do in life. Jacob still had Joseph in the back of the line, the place of preference—which the brothers understood as the front of the line. Joseph grew up as Jacob's favorite. And if the brothers had missed the message over the last eleven years since moving to Canaan, they got it now. You couldn't miss it. The coat made it clear. They deeply resented this visual reminder Joseph paraded on his back.

In fact, because of it, "they hated him" (Gen. 37:4).

Remember how you felt that Christmas when your sister opened the gift you wanted? Or when your brother got a T-bird for graduation and you got stuck with the family Nova? Fast-forward to today and ask yourself how it hits you when a co-worker gets a raise but you have done more work—or perhaps, *his* work? Or when a neighbor decorates her home from an unrestricted budget and you're gluing the peeling wallpaper back on the wall? We find ourselves kids again, pouting around the Christmas tree amid our piles of toys.

There's a reason Scripture has to command us not to covet. It's in our (fallen) nature. It's systemic. It's the kneejerk reaction of jerks. If we can't have more than others, at least we want it equal. But less than others? Uh, *no.*

Unfair situations do more than aggravate our sense of justice. They also pierce the thin veneer of our humility, and out oozes a malodorous pride called jealousy. Like the day laborers in Jesus's parable—hired at the beginning of the day—we resent the privileged loafer on whom the landowner dotes (see Matt. 20:1–15). Even though we get paid a full day's wage for our work, we begrudge the fact that someone else gets the same for sitting on their duff all day. As we read Jesus's parable, we line up in agreement with those who protest the inequitable pay. We've all experienced it. We hate unfairness. But we must recognize that from God's perspective, we *all* represent those hired at the end of the day—those who got something for nothing.

As we stand before the Father, we receive his generosity, not his equity. Unfair isn't so bad after all. God has doted on us far, far more than we deserve. He simply applies a different measure of grace to different people—for his sovereign purposes.

But it's grace all the same. Undeserved.

Jacob should have known better than to give favoritism to Joseph. After all, Jacob's own father, Isaac, had a favorite son too (and it wasn't Jacob, by the way). Had he forgotten? Jacob should have remembered the painful pangs he felt as the unloved son. He should have recalled how favoritism could rip a family apart. It had forever separated him from his mother—and it would soon remove him from Joseph.

When Jacob showered love on Joseph, he poured fuel on the fire of his other sons' jealousy. The brothers responded by hating the object of their father's affection. But Joseph himself would give them a new reason to hate him. This one came not from their father but from Joseph himself.

His dreams.

Joseph knew how his brothers felt about him. After all, they never spoke to him "on friendly terms" (Gen. 37:4). It was obvious. So why in the world he told them his bizarre dream about their sheaves bowing down in the field before his sheaf, I have no idea. Although Joseph never offered an interpretation of the dream, the meaning seemed plain enough to the brothers. They asked, "Are you actually going to reign over us?" (v. 8). To them, Joseph became more than the favored son with the special coat. Now he also seemed to gloat over his position—even in his sleep! Their hate only grew.

Dream number two drew a similar reaction from the brothers, and even Jacob chimed in with reproof: "What is this dream that you have had? Shall I and your mother and your brothers actually come to bow ourselves down before you to the ground?" (v. 10). Perhaps by "mother" Jacob meant his first wife, Leah, since Joseph's mother, Rachel, had already passed away. The whole family resented the dreams.

Joseph seemed to suffer from a mild case of naïveté. Most seventeen-year-olds do, you know. Remember seventeen? Oh, man. Hours in front of the mirror. Every hair in place. Every pimple a crisis. What to wear required a major decision. Why? Because peer pressure pushed hard. Approval was huge. No one liked oddballs.

That was Joseph. Brother oddball with the coat. The only people who admired Joseph were his baby brother and his old man. Those who *really* counted in Joseph's eyes, his older brothers, hated him.

How terribly isolated he must have felt. Who knows? Perhaps by sharing his dreams with his brothers he hoped to connect with them in some way.

But the dreams only served to drive them further apart. It was a no-win situation.

I have owned four Labradors through the years, and every one of them has had dreams. (Our current Lab snores louder than any human I've heard.) Most of these dog dreams look violent, even nightmarish. Muscles jerking, lips twitching, teeth bared, paws running, barking, growling—like some Freudian alter ego quivering on the living room floor. In fact, if I had connected their tails to a 220-volt cable and turned on the juice, I doubt they would have convulsed more violently. On one occasion I thought Rayah was literally having a seizure, so I touched her. She stopped trembling, looked at me, took a deep breath, and closed her glassy eyes again. Just a dream. No wonder Labradors snooze twelve to eighteen hours a day; they need rest from all that exhausting sleep!

I have often wondered what our dogs dream. I mean, all they know of the world comes from the backyard. What could be so exciting? A dog's dreams are frequent and violent, therefore comical—and insignificant.

Our own dreams get more attention. If we remember them when we awake, we find they usually reflect a slice of reality flavored with an offbeat imagination—kind of like Alice in some funky wonderland. (My wife designs houses in her dreams.) Have you ever wondered, *Why in the WORLD did I dream that?* Even though we seldom take our dreams seriously, they do mean more to us than dog dreams. At least we wonder *why* we dreamed them. Even weird dreams have reasons—whether they betray a fearful subconscious, a distressing memory, or just bad pizza from the night before.

Dreams in the Bible, however, often represented more than nocturnal brain waves. They served as a means of prophetic announcement from God.

Let me pause for a moment and note that while our dreams may have *reasons*, we need to guard against the urge to assign them *meaning*. What we think about when we sleep reflects who *we* are, indeed—but we have insufficient New Testament permission to interpret our dreams as direct revelation from God. The author of the book of Hebrews relates how God spoke in the Old Testament "to the fathers in the prophets in many portions and in many ways," then adds that God "in these last days has spoken to us in His Son" (Heb. 1:1–2). The New Testament records all God wants us to know about what Jesus said as well as how believers should live until Christ comes for us. New Testament authors repeatedly point us to Scripture—all its gaps notwithstanding—and not to some other means of hearing from God.

Although the Bible doesn't tell us everything we want to know, it does tell us all we need to know. It will always seem easier (and far more sensational) to be a mystic than to be biblically literate. Mystics don't wait to hear from God's Word in his timing. They don't live by faith. The direct line they claim to have with God is nothing but an expression of immaturity and impatience. God has already spoken. Are there exceptions, say on the mission field? Of course. We can't put God in a box. But exceptional experiences remain just that—and they don't endorse a new norm or standard for us. God's Word remains sufficient. We have the end of the story. We need no additional revelation. We just need to read, obey, and proclaim what we already have.

Joseph and his family, however, didn't have Bibles like we do. None! Not one scrap of Holy Writ. Instead, the Word of God came to people through a variety of means—dreams being one of them. Before Joseph, God spoke through dreams to Abraham, Abimelech, Jacob, and even Laban. As we move forward in Joseph's story, several more people will hear from God this way. And that's just in the book of Genesis.

In other words, Joseph's dreams meant more than the fantasies of a spoiled kid longing for approval. They represented prophecy— a revelation from God about the future. What did those dreams reveal?

Joseph would rule over the family.

Even though Joseph's dreams earned him the hatred of his brothers and a wrist slap from Jacob, his father knew what dreams could mean. He had dreamed too. He kept the dreams in mind, we're told.

But what happened next would cause them to disappear.

2

WHEN DREAMS
TURN INTO NIGHTMARES

*Here comes this dreamer! Now then, come and let us kill
him. . . . Then let us see what will become of his dreams!*

Genesis 37:19–20

The valley of Hebron where Jacob and his family sojourned
lay in the southern part of Canaan's hill country. South of
Hebron the hills sloped down to Beersheba and the barren
region of the Negev. Although high in elevation, Hebron couldn't
compare to the fertile fields that lay farther north near Shechem.
In the summertime even today, shepherds move their flocks north
to this same area to find grass sufficient for their flocks.

The brothers had taken the flock north to Shechem, and evidently they had stayed for some time.

Jacob dispatched Joseph to go and report back on the welfare
of the brothers and the flock. "I will go," Joseph answered. (Don't

you wish all teenagers answered like that?) I admire this young man's response. We see Joseph's godly character emerging. It's possible earlier he modeled faithfulness in bringing a bad report about his brothers. After all, he could have lied to get on his brothers' good side. It is hard to detect his motive back then, but here it's clear.

The trip would take Joseph about a week and require 130 miles of traveling alone. Furthermore, he knew his brothers hated him. He understood brutal words awaited him in Shechem. Joseph knew all that. Still, he would go.

He packed for what he knew would prove a tough assignment. But how tough? Oh, man; he had no idea.

Before saying goodbye, Joseph embraced his father, and Jacob would have kissed his boy to embarrassment. A prayer over the lad, a tearful parting, and he was off. Maybe even a final wave before the last bend in the road hid them from each other. One last farewell for a week.

And twenty-two years would pass before they would see each other again.

The sixty-five-mile trip to Shechem sounds rugged to us, but Joseph had an easy road to travel. "The Way of the Patriarchs" functioned as a well-worn highway that followed the watershed of the hill country and had served innumerable travelers for thousands of years. Joseph's great-granddad Abraham spent much of his life in Canaan wandering this ancient path, sojourning at places such as Shechem, Bethel and Ai, Hebron, and Beersheba. Joseph would have known the stories of each place, although he would pass only a few of the sites.

Some stops along the way already held tender memories for Joseph. When he saw Salem (ancient Jerusalem), Joseph would have remembered how Abraham traveled this way with Isaac to sacrifice him in the region of Mount Moriah. As he approached the place where his mother lay in her grave, Joseph would have remembered how she died there giving birth to his brother Benjamin. I wonder how long Joseph lingered, weeping over her memory. No doubt he looked forward to seeing the place again on his way home in a few days.

Farther along he passed Bethel, where his father had dreamed the vision of Jacob's ladder before leaving Canaan. Staring into the sky as he slept that night, Joseph may have imagined angels on the stairway to heaven. He must have pondered his own dreams in those many hours alone.

Just outside of Shechem, Joseph reached the property his father had acquired years earlier. He may have even drawn water from Jacob's well to replenish his supply. But looking across the fields, Joseph saw his brothers nowhere. Where could they have gone? He could still remember why the family had left Shechem, although he had been young at the time. As payback for the rape of their younger sister, Joseph's brothers Simeon and Levi had massacred every male in Shechem. To avoid further conflict, the family left the area.

Perhaps this was the reason Jacob had sent Joseph to check on the welfare of the brothers. After all, the last time they left here, the locals were understandably peeved. This may even be why the brothers had moved the flock on from Shechem and Joseph couldn't find them.

Whatever the reason for the brothers' absence, they had moved on without sending word as to their whereabouts, avoiding all accountability. But God knew where they were.

At this point, many of us in Joseph's sandals might have said, "Oh well, I tried." Then we would have hustled back south to the safety of Daddy, our conscience satisfied with a minimal effort.

But Joseph kept looking. His father had told him to check on the brothers and the flock. Having received information about the brothers from a chance bystander, Joseph took off for Dothan—another seventeen miles northwest. He found them there.

No doubt the brothers had enjoyed their break from Daddy's pet child. When they saw him coming in the distance, wearing that blasted coat, their adrenaline surged. To them, Joseph's tattling was one thing. And the coat inflamed their hatred. But his arrogant dreams? They broke the camel's back.

As they saw him coming, something snapped in their minds. All the anger, all the jealousy, all the frustration finally exploded into a scheme that promised to solve their problem.

"Let's kill him!"

Well, yeah, I guess that would do it. They intended to dispose of his corpse in a nearby cistern and then lie to their father that some "wild [literally *evil*] beast devoured him" (Gen. 37:20).

But Reuben stepped in with an alternative plan. "Shed no blood," he proposed. "Throw him into this pit that is in the wilderness" (v. 22). Still sounds pretty cruel. However, Reuben secretly intended to take Joseph back to Jacob. Maybe the big brother felt like he could get back in good with Dad after having blown it by sleeping with his father's wife (and his brothers' mother). Or perhaps, as the oldest brother, he felt responsible. Maybe he simply knew that to kill Joseph would be one step too far. Noble or selfish, whatever the reason, it worked. They chose to spare Joseph's life.

When Joseph arrived, the first thing the brothers did was strip him of the coat that separated him from them. First things first. Then they "threw him" into the pit. The original term for *threw* means just that. They roughed him up.

Next, if you can believe it, they sat down for a picnic. The old Puritan Thomas Fuller wondered how they could say grace before the meal. It probably never crossed their minds. Like the adulteress of Proverbs 30:20, they ate and wiped their mouths and said, "I have done no wrong." Ironically, they planned to claim an evil beast devoured Joseph, and yet it was they who sat down to eat. The same root word in Hebrew connects the two verbs, as if to ask, "Who's the evil beast here, guys? Who's really devouring Joseph?"

Just as they had seen Joseph coming up the Dothan Valley from the south, so the brothers could also see a caravan coming from the north. Ishmaelite traders from Gilead rode camels loaded with aromatic gum, balm, and myrrh. The highway from Gilead crossed the Jordan River and followed the Harod Valley west until it merged with the famous international highway. This superhighway stretched from Syria to Egypt and forked in three directions through the Mount Carmel range. One of these roads led through the Dothan Valley, right where Joseph's brothers were devouring their picnic.

Seeing the traders sparked an idea in Judah. If the brothers simply killed Joseph, or let him rot in the cistern, what would they gain beyond his absence? Why not make some cash by selling him as a slave to these traders? The brothers would be rid of him just the same. But they would also get some easy money.

The idea took root. They flagged down the Ishmaelites.

In spite of Joseph's begging and crying, they sold the dreamer to the traders, and the brothers pocketed two shekels each. As the merchants made their way southwest through the Dothan Valley, Joseph's cries grew more and more faint. Finally, they could hear nothing.

Silence.

But his screams would echo in their heads for years. They thought they had gotten rid of Joseph, but he was with them now more than ever. He was inside their heads. He was a pebble wedged in the sandals of their consciences.

Evidently, Reuben had left during the meal, perhaps to tend the flock. He had not been there for the slave sale. Remember, it was Reuben who saved Joseph's life by keeping the others from killing him. Reuben had suggested hurling him into the pit. Reuben planned to return Joseph to Jacob. So when Reuben saw the empty cistern and discovered what had happened, he felt desperate—and responsible. He couldn't return to Jacob empty-handed.

The brothers returned to their "evil beast" scheme. They sought to substantiate it by adding another hue to Joseph's coat of many colors. Red. They dipped the tunic in goat's blood in order to deceive their father into believing that a beast had devoured the boy. Pretty clever. After all, they had learned from their parents that when life gets tough you take matters into your own hands. The boys were chips off the old block. They would chisel the chiseler. They would deceive the deceiver. It was Cain and Abel all over again. For all practical purposes, the brothers did destroy Joseph. They sold him as a slave, and slavery was as good as a death sentence.

In order to conceal the deed, they would have to commit another sin by lying to their father. This was risky. After all, Reuben's conscience already panged him. What if one brother cracked and spilled the beans? What if one of them shared the truth with his wife?

From this point forward, no brother could trust another. They had a new family secret to keep.

Their alibi in tow, they pointed their flock toward home. In the few days from Dothan to Hebron, I'm sure words were few. Miles and miles with bleating sheep as the only sound. Their throats were quiet, but their consciences screamed.

Places they saw along the way hid ghosts that would have added to their burden. They saw Shechem, where they had brutally taken matters into their own hands. At Bethel, they passed the place where God had changed their father's name from Jacob ("deceiver") to Israel ("one who strives with God"); there God had repeated the command to "be fruitful and multiply" (Gen. 35:11), something the selling of Joseph hardly helped to accomplish. Making their way south, they passed Salem and saw Moriah, where their great-grandfather Abraham had spilled a ram's blood in place of his son's. The bloody tunic they carried marked a contrast between Abraham's faith while in an impossible situation and their own self-will in their incident.

40

But the final ghost would have appeared as they approached the pillar that marked Rachel's grave. The brothers remembered when Joseph's mother had died and how the boy had wept—not to mention the bitter tears that had flowed from their father. They had just heard Joseph's weeping again at Dothan. They were about to hear Jacob's in Hebron. Passing Rachel's tomb would have been a difficult moment of déjà vu.

From a distance, the father saw his sons approaching. A prayer of thanks no doubt arose from the old man. But as they drew near, Jacob noticed a conspicuous absence. He counted only ten. The brothers came close and spoke first.

"We found this," they blurted, "please examine it to see whether it is your son's tunic or not" (37:32). Wow, what tact. Even their thin fib betrayed their hatred. They refer to him as "your son," not "Joseph"—and certainly not "our brother."

As the old man's trembling hands reached for the garment, he instantly recognized the coat and assumed the worst: "A wild beast has devoured him; Joseph has surely been torn to pieces!" (v. 33). As Jacob dropped his staff, his hips went slack and he fell to his knees, tore his clothes, and scooped dirt onto his head.

The brothers must have felt relief mixed with an unexpected, stabbing shame. The lie worked, yes. They were off the hook. The words were exactly what they had hoped their father would say. But his grief-stricken response revealed they had absolutely crushed their father's spirit. By selling Joseph, they had hoped to rid themselves of the painful reality that Jacob loved Joseph the most. Instead, they intensified the fact. Their father's extreme reaction only confirmed it.

They had heard their father cry many times before. But this time it was different. This time the brothers *owned* the grief. Every time their father howled, they felt their own consciences wrench. They knew their betrayal, lying, and jealousy were the cause of his pain.

Day after day, the father wept openly and wore sackcloth on his loins. All efforts by the sons to comfort him only added to their deception. Jacob refused any effort at consolation. After all, a wild beast had ripped his son to shreds.

Don't you find it strange that the brothers "found" only the tunic? No other clothes? No body parts to bury? Don't wild beasts eat varicolored tunics as well as undergarments? It didn't add up. And let's not forget that Jacob himself had also killed a goat in order to deceive *his* father. Inherited trickery. True poetic irony. And sad.

But hey, what about Joseph's dreams? Jacob knew firsthand that God often spoke in dreams. Why didn't Jacob believe God's revelation over a bloody garment produced by sons prone to lying? Even if Joseph *was* dead, couldn't God bring him back to life to fulfill his promise—just as Abraham expected would happen after he planned to sacrifice Isaac (see Heb. 11:19)?

But for Jacob, circumstantial evidence tipped the scales against all logic or faith. Natural circumstances seemed much more compelling than God's revelation.

Joseph was gone. But his empty chair at the table found a new occupant. The elephant in the room took his seat. A large, foul-smelling animal with an unforgiving gaze—the big family secret the brothers didn't dare discuss. An elephant joined the tribes of Israel.

Between the incessant wailing of Jacob and the chronic stench of the beast with the trunk, the brothers' burden must have seemed unbearable. Their annoyance with Joseph's presence was replaced by something far worse.

The misery of his absence.

I'm convinced some company today could make a killing if it had the guts to market dysfunctional greeting cards. Most birthday or holiday cards gush with flowery sentiments such as, "To the greatest father in the world," or, "Mom, you are my best friend." Yeah, well, what if they weren't? What if your dad was an angry jerk and your mother abused you? What if your brother back-stabbed you and stole the inheritance? Where are the greeting cards for reality? Just once I'd like to see a card that reads, "Mom, you blew it . . . but I love you anyway. Happy Mother's Day." It'll never happen.

Even if such cards existed, few people would have the cruelty to send them. So instead we shop for cards that are blank inside and do our best to scrawl some positive words. There are no easy solutions. Only godly ones. After all, on some level we all deserve to open dysfunctional envelopes since we each contribute our own family defects.

Most children grow up seeing their dysfunction as normal. Multiple divorces, sibling cruelties, hush-hush affairs, cover-up abortions, recurring abuses, and parental favoritisms all make up the experience of our childhoods. Blended families often hit kids the hardest. They're expected to get along and deal with it, but figuring out *how* to deal with it breeds its own dysfunction. Even if we were blessed to have a home in which our parents stayed together and where peace (not perfection) generally existed, all it takes is a glance at a friend, a church member, or a grandparent to see dysfunction in the raw. We cannot escape it. We all know it on some level.

In a way, I can relate to Joseph. I grew up with a variety of stepparents, stepsiblings, half-siblings, and even occasional live-in parental concubines. I had two families, one on either end of Texas, and a monthly airplane trip as the bridge. As strange as it sounds, the only times I ever saw my biological parents in the same room occurred during the holiday handoff and at my wedding. Because I had never known it otherwise, it was the epitome of strangeness to experience my parents together. It was just . . . odd. So much so it felt wrong when we three were in the same room together. Just a feeling, I know—not a fact—but the emotions were severe. The closest thing I can compare it to is my first visit to a foreign country. Two worlds collided, and I didn't speak the language.

All this to say, *normal is what you know*. Even when it's abnormal.

We seldom outgrow the memories that brand such pain on our hearts—even after God brings healing. Most kids have seen enough relational carnage by the age of seventeen that they make bold promises to themselves. *I will never be like my parents. My family will be different*. Or more dramatically, *I will never marry*. But the fact is, regardless of the extreme oaths we make in moments of frustration, our parents' examples train us to be like them. We are hardwired to repeat the failures.

It takes more than promises to break the cycle, to unravel the knots, and to dislodge the dysfunction from our hearts. It takes years of intentional, brutally challenging work. Sometimes it takes even more severe measures.

That's where God steps in.

⌒

While Jacob wept for his son in Hebron, Joseph cried on the back of a camel headed for Egypt. Or more likely, as he was dragged on a leash for a long, long walk. Through tears he had seen the hills on either side of the Dothan Valley give way to the broad Plain of Sharon beside the Mediterranean Sea. Familiar surroundings surrendered to the unfamiliar. The international highway paralleled the coast miles inland in order to avoid the mosquitos and swamps beside the sea. Near Joppa, the highway forked west and followed the coastline more closely. Most likely, Joseph had never seen the sea before. Certainly not this close. No hope of visiting the coast would ever have included this scenario. The continuous crashing of waves and the salty gusts only added to the desperation of everything unfamiliar.

Think of those times you spent the night in a hotel or at someone's home and you woke up disoriented by the strange surroundings. Once the mental fog cleared—*Oh yeah, I'm in a hotel room*—you relaxed and even laughed at yourself. Reality brought relief. But that didn't happen for Joseph.

Just imagine. The first few days on the way to Egypt you wake up startled by the unfamiliar, only to remember it's worse than you first supposed. You're being kidnapped. Your hands and feet are raw and bleeding from pulling against the ropes. Your gut gnaws with thirst and hunger. You're sick from eating moldy food scraps. Your father and family are gone. You relive the horror of your brothers' betrayal. Your mind echoes with their hateful words, the looks in their eyes, their brutal bullying, their cold resolution to be rid of you. You stared into the faces of family but saw total strangers. Imagine, your own brothers—selling you for money!

In the journey from Dothan to Egypt, Joseph endured two long weeks of these rude awakenings. He had no clue that back home a gory tunic had duped his father. For all Joseph knew, Jacob would wrench the truth from his bad-boy sons and dispatch a swift rescue party. Joseph may have even looked over his shoulder, back toward Canaan, waiting and hoping. But the rescue never came. Canaan had disappeared.

Words fail to relate the utter aloneness that washes over you when family or best friends wear the faces of strangers. The feeling of abandonment or betrayal is at first, more than anything, confusing. Disbelief might better describe the emotion. As the reality of the disloyalty sinks in, disbelief becomes desperation—and eventually it erodes into heartache as palpable as a migraine. When the permanence of it all becomes plain, hopelessness and despair unpack their bags and settle in—eating everything in your pantry. Maybe you have experienced the feelings of betrayal. I have, and

I'm telling you—there is no more desperate, alone, and fearful place. Especially when Job's counselors show up to explain what you did wrong to make all that happen to you. It's like having rocks in your heart. If not for God's presence, you'd go nuts.

As I read Joseph's story, one phrase continues to chafe my brain. I can't escape the words. The brothers made the statement along with their plans to get rid of Joseph. Consider carefully what they said: "Then let us see what will become of his dreams!" (Gen. 37:20). At first, the sentence seems like little more than a spiteful jab from jealous brothers. And from a purely horizontal perspective, their statement makes sense. Joseph dreamed the family would one day bow in homage to him—that he would rule over them. The brothers' plan to get rid of Joseph cut the legs off those dreams. Pretty tough to rule over the family when you're a slave in a foreign land, you know?

For the brothers, all it took to remove the stench of those dreams was to remove the dreamer. Problem solved. Let's see what happens to his dreams now.

I guess it's possible the brothers failed to see Joseph's dreams as divine revelation. Likely it never crossed their minds. Even if it had, they quickly extinguished the thought. After all, who wants to bow in homage before a younger sibling? Nobody lines up to defer to someone less qualified, younger, and doted on as Daddy's favorite. Buried in their statement we see deep roots of envy, independence, self-interest, and the taproot of it all—pride.

But whether or not they comprehended the source of Joseph's dreams, they certainly understood that they were trying to thwart them. That much their statement makes clear.

Not only were the brothers removing Joseph's offensive dreams but they were also eradicating the object of their father's love. This was the real issue, wasn't it? That's why they stripped off Joseph's tunic as soon as he arrived. By doffing the multicolored coat, the brothers betrayed their true motives. Their jealousy of

Joseph wasn't envy of his great relationship with their father. Are you kidding?

Each one of them had his own set of dreams—*daydreams* might better term their ambitions.

Ironically, their dreams were the same as Joseph's. I don't mean their dreams came from God. Rather, each brother envisioned himself as ruling the others. They weren't jealous for justice. They were envious of Joseph's lucky lot in life. They wanted to wear the coat. They wanted Jacob's favor. They wanted what being loved the most meant. Authority. Power. Influence. Greatness. Reuben tipped his hand to this when he slept with his stepmom; he was hoping to step up to Daddy's position prematurely.

But Jacob gave Joseph preeminence as the firstborn of the favorite wife. Joseph was the heir apparent, and the older brothers chafed at that choice because each wanted it for himself.

Waiting on God never entered the minds of these young men. Discerning God's will, trusting him to make his choice, allowing providence to have its way, and finding contentment in whatever place God designed for them? All totally foreign notions.

There is never room for the will of God in a heart filled with self—with one's own ambitions. Instead, God's will is assumed. God's desires sound inaudible against the din of daydreams. Maybe that's why Jesus reminded us of the greatest commandment of all—to "love the Lord your God with *all* your heart and with *all* your soul and with *all* your mind and with *all* your strength" (Mark 12:30 NIV, emphasis added). The word *all* leaves no room for rivals.

Anything that crowds out our love for God is—let's call it what it is—an idol. We will not wait on God if we don't love him supremely.

Thousands of years didn't improve human ambition. Even Jesus's disciples competed for who would be the "greatest." Two of them even had the gall to solicit Christ for the top seats in the kingdom of God. (Want to see someone's character in the raw? Just watch how they act around important people.) Jesus taught his power-hungry disciples that the way up is down. The greatest among them was to be the least. Two thousand years after Jesus, we still fumble that principle. And two thousand years before Jesus, Jacob's sons failed to get it too.

If you think about it, getting rid of Joseph solved nothing. Each brother still had ten other brothers as competition. So who wears the tunic now? One rival down, ten to go. "Let us see what will become of his dreams!" Yes, and let's see what will become of the other brothers' dreams. At least Joseph was honest about his. The truth is, each brother had the same dream as Joseph.

Their father, Jacob, knew full well God could speak in dreams. He had seen it occur in his own life a number of times! And yet a bloody tunic proved more convincing to Jacob than his own experience with God? Amazingly, yes.

Why didn't Jacob simply see these events as a test? I'll tell you why. Jacob had a different taproot God would have to jerk loose. Because Jacob refused all comfort in his wailing, he had no one who could speak into the real reasons for his grief. Often the authority role handicaps a leader's recognition of serious blind spots. As the one in authority, Jacob permitted no one around him the freedom to be honest and say, "Jacob, you are failing to follow God's Word because you are idolizing your affection for your son. Your nepotism has blinded you to wisdom."

There was a lot of refusing going on. The brothers refused to serve Joseph. Jacob refused any comfort about losing Joseph. Both refusals betrayed the same response to God's Word. Although one stemmed from pride and another from inordinate affection, their roots fed the same base desire—a demand to have one's own way, regardless of what God has said.

Jacob's self-inflicted wounds came from point-blank fire. Idol worship always backfires—or more accurately, fires backward. Clinging to an idol reminds me of the idiocy in the mind of a suicide bomber. He straps to himself what symbolizes his commitment, passion, and beliefs—and yet, his misguided devotion blows him to bits.

"Then let us see what will become of his dreams!" Jacob never heard this phrase spoken but his actions betrayed the fact that he fully believed it.

Although the big picture of God's providence overshadows the story, God was also in the details of personal growth—accomplishing, as only God can do, his purposes on both levels. God would use circumstances to directly challenge the sons' desire to look out for number one. The Lord would also use the situation to directly challenge Jacob's refusal to trust him with his favorite sons.

And what about Joseph? Was God going to teach him anything as well? If so, what? I wonder if God asked Joseph to share his dreams, or if that sharing represented any weakness on his part. We'll never know. Joseph would later exhibit so much restraint in Egypt, so much wisdom in keeping his mouth shut until the right time, that it does seem strange he would tell his brothers and father what they were unready to hear. Perhaps there was a youthful naïveté from which Joseph had to grow. We've all been there.

But there was certainly more than that. God was working on Joseph's heart, although it's tough to know to what degree or for what purpose God "tested" Joseph. But he did (see Ps. 105:16–19).

Remember, the gaps in Scripture mean that what God selected to record has his reasons all over it. God wants us to read this story because it's not only about Joseph's family.

It's about us.

If we're honest, we're all somewhere in these pages. We identify with the brothers, the father, and of course, with Joseph.

Joseph must have thought, *Wait a minute, God, this wasn't part of the deal. The dream you gave me about my brothers didn't include them selling me to a foreign land! Did I miss something here?* Joseph knew his dreams were of God. But circumstances directly challenged that promise. So would he give up on that revelation? The rest of the narrative sets out to bring resolution to what seemed like a contradiction.

"Then let us see what will become of his dreams!" The brothers' words may seem like a throwaway statement, but they provide the tension for the entire story.

May I take that idea further? The brothers' words reveal the tension for our entire lives.

It's the same struggle we face when the promises God gives us are challenged by the life God gives us. They seem to contradict. We read Scripture, and God's Word seems clear. But as we face challenges we never imagined possible, suddenly the verses feel as unreliable as last night's crazy dream—or worse, they seem as laughable as dog dreams.

We think we understand the principles of Scripture—until we get shoved headlong into a pit. It's really tough to sing, "Rejoice in the Lord always," when you're strapped sideways to the back of a camel. That's why the hardest part of dealing with any stabbing disappointment in life isn't the pain itself as much as it is the spiritual confusion. Why would God allow this?

Ultimately, our problem is with God. But we don't say that. We'll point to people as the reason pain lurks in our lives. Parents, bosses, children, and spouses—and even the devil has his part to play. If God would only bring relief, all would be well. It's a crisis of faith, not of circumstance.

I love that the Bible includes reality in the lives of its spiritual giants. Jacob and Joseph represent only two. Moses also knew God had sent him to deliver his people, but after a hard experience one day, Moses blurted, "You have not delivered Your people at all" (Exod. 5:23). Consider this question: "How long, O LORD? Will You forget me forever?" (Ps. 13:1). Sooner or later, this psalmist's question finds its way to the lips of every believer in God. A question like that sounds almost heretical—if it hadn't come from King David. This is how David *felt*, but it isn't what he *believed*.

We often feel what we don't believe, don't we? That's our tension—putting our faith in front of our feelings. These biblical giants were people just like us. Weak, struggling, dependent, and confused about how to reconcile reality with truth.

Our present pain seems so permanent. We want immediate relief or we immediately lose heart. We hate red lights. We hate gaps. We hate waiting on God.

Waiting on God feels like living a dysfunctional spiritual life, like making the mistake of trying to "get used to" an abusive situation, or an angry spouse, or an absent parent. Because we have promises from God he seems to have forgotten, we feel we're the losers in a waiting game played with One who has infinite patience.

But waiting on God is not dysfunctional. It is normal.

When Jesus told the apostles of his impending death and resurrection, they completely rejected the cross. Their fixation with only the glorious parts of the Messiah blinded their vision because they refused to face reality.

We do the same thing. We focus on how the Christian life "ought" to be—and we stick our fingers in our ears at those parts we don't want to hear, those verses like, "take up your cross and follow me." *Um, no thanks.* As if the tough parts of the Christian life are electives. We have adopted the lifestyle of a tourist who wants to see only the highlights of the city. Forget all the back alleys of London. Show us Westminster Abbey. We tend to interpret our Christianity as we want it rather than as God reveals it. Then God shows us how the Christian life really is. It's not as though he duped us. Rather, it's that we have selective hearing. He told us the truth; we just wouldn't hear it all.

So we're surprised when hard times are part of normal. In reality, the surprise should come if we do *not* experience trouble (see 1 Cor. 7:28; 1 Thess. 3:3–4; 1 Pet. 4:12; 1 John 3:13).

Between our reading of God's promises and the time when we enjoy the fulfillment of those promises comes a "time of testing" (Luke 8:13 NIV). This testing, according to Jesus's parable, comes after the seed gets sown. After we receive God's Word, a gap of testing comes to see if we'll believe it. It happens to everybody. And even when we remain faithful to God's Word, that won't necessarily remove the test.

Joseph had done nothing to deserve this. In fact, he was faithful, and yet his own flesh and blood betrayed him. If we live a moral life just so God will reward us with colored coats, we will be disappointed one day as that blessing is stripped away and we find ourselves in a pit. The question we should ask is not why we don't have more blessings but why we have any at all. As Jeremiah asked, "Why should any living mortal, or any man, offer complaint in view of his sins?" (Lam. 3:39).

When we pray for God to bring relief, or change, or a certain result from a challenging situation, we have to remember that what we're asking God to do—even though it may be completely within the bounds of Scripture—comes from a limited perspective. We look at the situation and evaluate it in such a way as to think, *Lord, bring about this result in my character. Help me be more loving, patient, self-controlled, and so on.* Obviously, God wants us to be these things, but he may have another result in mind altogether.

He sees the blind spots in our character—those areas we don't even know to pray for. So he shapes the situation to unearth the defects buried deeply beneath layers of immature jealousies, lusts, and longings for relief.

Sometimes God's greatest acts of love come in saying no to our requests because he wants to give us much, much more than answers to third-grade questions. He wants to grow us up to be like his Son—and the Father will never stop this relentless pursuit in our lives (see Rom. 8:29; Phil. 1:6).

It's amazing that the same Peter who bristled against Jesus's cross—"Lord! This shall never happen to You!"—would later write, "Do not be surprised at the fiery ordeal among you" (Matt. 16:22; 1 Pet. 4:12). What transformed this man who wanted nothing but glory from Jesus into a man willing to be crucified upside down for Christ in Rome?

Failure, heartbreak, and bitter tears, that's what.

God allowed Peter to experience reality. It wasn't that Peter's ambitions were wrong. After all, Jesus did promise the disciples that they would reign on thrones (see Matt. 19:28). Peter's problem came in how those dreams were to come about. The cross never figured into Peter's plans, and so every single time Jesus brought it up Peter bristled and forcefully rejected it. In order for him to become free of the fear of the cross, he had to experience God's faithfulness through it. We're the same.

A broad chasm stretches between the God we want and the God who is. As tough as it sounds, the only way to bridge this gap is the cross. Or, I should say, *your* cross. And my cross. We all have one—tailor-made to fit.

Our cross isn't something that graces our necks for ornamentation. It's something that splinters our shoulders as we drag it through life. The cross that Jesus commands us to take up does its work in us bit by bit, every day, to rub, rub, rub away the tough veneer that's calcified over our hearts.

We think our problem is with God, but remember, God is perfect. Our problem is really with ourselves.

God never asked Joseph if he'd like a trip to Egypt. He was tied and taken. Providence takes no votes on the itinerary.

One day Joseph enjoyed the comforts and advantages as the favored son. The next day his wrists bled raw from his slave bindings. The tasty delicacies of his Hebrew home were replaced with moldy Ishmaelite leftovers. Well-known pathways disappeared and unfamiliar sights emerged along a strange road. He swapped a privileged position in his large family for a hardscrabble life as a slave in a stranger's home. Joseph's whole world got jerked out from under him. In fact, his last memory of *anything* familiar included echoes of his brothers' laughter at his pleadings for mercy. His dreams had turned into nightmares.

All in the course of one day, Joseph lost everything. Imagine that for a moment. Everything familiar—gone.

Including his dysfunctional family.

Sometimes it may be helpful for God to remove us from our situation if it is so freakishly dysfunctional we need another place to meet and grow with him. When dysfunction is all we know, we think it's normal.

Joseph was hardwired to fail because of the family from which he came. God removed Joseph from that context in order to shape him into the godly man he would become. Did Joseph see that at the time? Absolutely not. Neither do we.

Like Joseph, we find ourselves taken on compulsory journeys by God. They usually start, ironically, by unpacking. By removing those props in our lives that we've learned to rely on instead of God. Off come the multicolored coats. Away go the doting daddies we've come to need. Distant now are the brothers who betrayed us. Enter a strange world where no one speaks our language and we know no one.

No one except God.

A sovereign God never asks us what we'd prefer. We only follow and discover the path he lights step by step. Choice enters the picture only as we decide how to respond to God's leading. As with Adam and Eve, the choice is given us to eat the fruit or not to eat. But we are not given the choice of whether eating is right or wrong—or of removing the fruit altogether. Like Jesus in Gethsemane, we pray, "Father, if You are willing, remove this cup from Me; yet not My will, but Yours be done" (Luke 22:42).

As Joseph entered Egypt, we read, "The LORD was with Joseph" (Gen. 39:2).

That truth extends beyond Joseph's life to ours. God is with us. Often that truth is all we know. He is with us, not to answer questions but to comfort us as he takes us to a place that teaches us to trust him by forcing us to do so. We really learn no other way.

At the outset, we never would have chosen these strange gaps of God's sovereignty in our lives. But in the end, we never would have missed them.

Thank God he keeps secrets.

3

SATISFACTION ON HOLD

How then could I do this great evil and sin against God?

Genesis 39:9

My grandmother used to make mouthwatering fried apricot pies. Three bites would do the job. Just thinking about those little pastries gets the juices flowing in my mouth!

Once when I was a kid, I ate more than my share of those delicious pies. That night around 1:00 a.m., the Grim Reaper came calling. I awoke with a tight burning in my stomach. I had never suffered heartburn before, so I mistook the indigestion for—no joke—hunger pangs!

You can guess what I did. I hurried downstairs and relieved the kitchen counter of a few more fried pies. Problem solved. A couple of hours later, I woke up even hungrier! So I tried it again. See the pattern? If I had only known my real problem, I would have headed to the medicine cabinet instead of the kitchen cabinet.

Here's the terrible irony: *I was trying to relieve my pain by eating the very thing that caused it.*

God made us to hunger. The pangs we feel in life come from his original design. He also created, along with that need, what we require to satisfy the hunger. Some pangs are true needs, others are godly desires, and still others are just flat-out misdirected lusts. At times, the burning we feel can make it seem impossible to tell the difference between lust and longing. But this much we can know for certain: whatever our hunger, each of our pangs finds its origin—and its solution—in God's design.

Given the choice, we want to do what's right. We want God's solutions to our physical and emotional pangs. The problem? Most godly solutions require *waiting*. Long gaps of delayed gratification make temptation so tempting. Let's face it. One of the biggest tugs of temptation comes from its immediacy.

Idling at the red light of God's will, we white-knuckle the steering wheel and wait for a signal from the Lord. We do our best not to mistake the gaps for God's apathy or his cruelty. As the days and months and years drag on, our needs feel bigger and bigger. We begin to see any solution—good or bad—as God's provision, and temptation's alternatives often seem irresistible. The fried pies are always downstairs.

But a funny thing happens after we sacrifice our integrity on the altar of impatience and convenience. Instead of satisfying our God-given pangs, temptation's quick fixes only intensify the cravings. They only fuel our desire for more—and never truly satisfy.

It's a vicious cycle of desperately seeking to satisfy our pain by pursuing the very thing that's causing it.

We barely begin Joseph's story when, without warning, Genesis takes a hard left turn.

The chapter that follows Joseph's journey to Egypt seems sort of misplaced. Almost as if Moses wasn't paying attention to the flow of the narrative. How in the world does a story about Judah leaving home and his subsequent family problems fit here? What does this odd parenthesis in Joseph's story have to do with Joseph? To be honest, very little—it seems at first. That's because we're asking the wrong question.

The better question is: What does Joseph's story have to do with Genesis—or better still—with the whole Bible?

As I mentioned earlier, the story of Joseph reveals God's providence to accomplish his good purposes when evil events seem to threaten them. This section of the Bible chronicles how God preserved the line of Judah, from whom the Messiah would come (see Matt. 1:1–3). That's why Moses introduces Joseph's narrative this way: "These are the records of the generations of *Jacob*" (Gen. 37:2, emphasis added). Jacob's name here seems like a misprint until we realize, on a grand scale, Joseph's story has much more than Joseph as its goal. It reveals God preserving Jacob's line through Judah. God simply used Joseph to make it happen.

"And it came about at that time," Genesis 38 begins, "that Judah departed from his brothers and visited a certain Adullamite" (v. 1). Why did Judah leave home? Probably because Hebron had too many ghosts haunting its halls. The memories of what he and his brothers had done to Joseph seemed inescapable. Every time they looked in each other's eyes they saw the deed. Every mournful cry from their father, Jacob, brought echoes of Joseph's pitiful pleadings in the Dothan Valley.

Judah could stomach it all no longer. Surely the elephant in the room would stay with the majority in Hebron. So Judah left.

He departed, or literally "went down," to Adullam—a descent of about fifteen miles from the top of the hill country into its foothills. Judah went to stay with his friend Hirah, but the text focuses on Judah's decision to marry a Canaanite woman. In a mere three verses, she bears him as many sons.

This chapter occurred "at that time," meaning during Joseph's sojourn in Egypt, and it represents many years. Remember, the Bible has gaps, and these first few verses trace Judah's marriage, the birth of his sons, and their growth to becoming husbands themselves.

The plot thickens when Judah chooses Tamar, presumably another Canaanite, to marry his eldest son in order to carry on the family line. But the Lord put that son to death because of his wickedness. Judah then tells his next son to marry her "and raise up offspring for your brother" (v. 8). This sounds odd to us, but it represented a custom in that day that later would find its affirmation in Scripture (see Deut. 25:5–10). The levirate marriage required that the brother of the dead husband marry his widow "in order to raise up the name of the deceased on his inheritance, so that the name of the deceased will not be cut off from his brothers" (Ruth 4:10).

However, when Judah's second son married Tamar and lay with her, he spilled his semen on the ground to prevent conception. This was so that the inheritance of the firstborn would fall to him instead of to his brother's "offspring." So God took this son's life as well! (See how Jacob's family's deception wormed its way from generation to generation?)

Judah feared that his final son would also die, so he gave Tamar an excuse that the boy needed first to grow up—and then she could marry him. Judah's refusal to give up his youngest son was rooted in fear. (Spoiler alert: that theme will come up again soon.)

Years passed, and Judah's wife passed on. The text simply states she died, and after some time, Judah "recovered from his grief"

(Gen. 38:12 NIV). But even though his wife died, Judah's desire for sexual intimacy didn't die. If marriage provides God's protection against sexual impurity (see 1 Cor. 7:9), what happens when that provision disappears? Does God suddenly furnish the spiritual gift of singleness to widows and widowers? Self-control will always be a fruit of the Spirit.

It's always joyful when God replaces something painful with something wonderful. Or when he provides for a need in a context of lack. But what about when God takes away something we enjoy—or even something we need? Or when he allows something bad to overrun something good? Can we then say what Job said: "Naked I came from my mother's womb, and naked I will depart. The LORD gave and the LORD has taken away; may the name of the LORD be praised" (Job 1:21 NIV)?

Let's be honest. During the times when the Lord takes something away from us, it's easy to feel duped. As if God were some kind of drug pusher, giving free samples and then removing them after the cravings have their hooks in our hearts. The Lord's generosity in these times can be misunderstood as cruelty. Rather than praise God for the time we enjoyed his blessings, we can grow to resent his sovereign prerogative to confiscate them.

During the times of removal, we discover, sadly, that Satan's accusation is often right on the money: "Does Job fear God for nothing?" (Job 1:9 NIV). Slip your name in the place of Job and see how accurate the statement sounds: "Does *Wayne* fear God for nothing?" Honestly, I'd really hate to find out.

What do our raw emotions reveal about our hearts when God takes away something wonderful? When the Lord gives and then takes away, we can betray an inordinate affection for the gift rather than for the Giver. Our reaction after the removal could reveal that we view God as One who merely dispenses blessings rather than One who has as his primary concern our holiness and spiritual growth.

61

It's hard, but it's true: sometimes God removes good things from our lives for our good. If we find ourselves constantly waiting on God only to bring us into another season of blessing, it may be that the initial blessing only came to reveal how addicted to blessings we have become.

There is a huge difference between waiting on God's blessings and waiting on God. We may feel it's the same, but it isn't.

Judah may have thought he needn't wait on God for sexual gratification. Or, more likely, maybe the Lord never entered his mind in that moment of temptation. After all, when we're grieving anything in life, if we don't run to God for comfort, we will turn somewhere else for consolation, distraction, or satisfaction.

Plenty of time had passed, and Tamar saw that Judah had yet to give his youngest son to her as a husband—as he should have. So in a bold move, she disguised herself as a prostitute and lured the sexually vulnerable widower into bed.

From our New Testament perspective, it seems hard to see Tamar's actions in a positive light. After all, putting it bluntly, she seduced her father-in-law into having sex with her by acting the part of a whore. She deceived him to get what she wanted. She pulled the ace of deception out of the family's card deck. Judah played the joker.

However, the motive behind her actions was anything but sensual. Her deed reflected her right to bear an heir by the nearest of kin to her dead husband. Judah had refused to comply with that right—a mistake he would later admit (see Gen. 38:26). So Tamar made her move based on what she knew of Judah's character.

Tamar's ruse on Judah finds an uncanny resemblance with his mother Leah's apparent deception of Jacob on their wedding night (see Gen. 29:23). Jacob, the deceiver, had met his match in his uncle Laban. Jacob contracted to work for Laban seven years in order to marry his younger daughter, Rachel. But after the time was up—and after a wedding night that must have had really, really dim lighting—Jacob rolled over in bed the next morning to see weak-eyed Leah instead of the curvaceous Rachel. Surprise! I love the way the NASB translates it: "Behold, it was Leah!" (v. 25). *Behold* is right. It may be the greatest double take in the Bible.

Still determined to have his prize, Jacob agreed to work another seven years for Laban in exchange for an immediate wedding to Rachel. Evidently, Jacob assumed the pleasure of the beautiful Rachel would outweigh the agony of polygamy—and marriage to two sisters at the same time. If the wrenching realities of daily life wouldn't make it plain enough to those who later would read Jacob's story, God would make it even plainer. Moses, the same author who recorded Jacob marrying two sisters in each other's lifetime, also codified God's later prohibition from doing so (see Lev. 18:18). The principle extends beyond polygamy to any sexual expression outside of God's provision of marriage.

Immorality never delivers what it promises. Judah knew this story about his dad, but he didn't learn the lesson. He had to discover it the hard way.

When Judah first saw Tamar, he assumed she was a common "harlot." As payment for her services, Judah promised her a young goat. In the meantime, he agreed to let her keep as security his staff and the cord around his neck, which carried his seal. That's like handing her his driver's license! When Judah's friend Hirah later went to deliver the goat, he tried to sidestep the stigma of inquiring about a harlot and asked instead the whereabouts of the "temple prostitute"—a higher-class woman than your garden-variety whore. Of course, neither occupation honored God, and the Bible would later condemn both types of prostitution (see Deut. 22:21; 23:17–18).

In a moment of impulse and weakness, Judah chose to gratify his sexual pangs in a way that didn't wait on God. He yielded to the temptation without resistance, knowing the whole time what he was doing was wrong.

But it backfired. Tamar got pregnant.

Months later, when Tamar's pregnancy began to show, Judah discovered that it came about as a result of harlotry. Enraged, he commanded her execution! Tamar simply pulled Judah's driver's license from her purse and sent his seal and cord to him with these words: "I am with child by the man to whom these things belong. . . . Please examine and see, whose . . . are these?" (Gen. 38:25).

Judah's exposure as a hypocrite pulled from him a confession. He admitted he should have given her his youngest son as a husband and annulled his order for her execution.

Just as Judah's great-grandfather Abraham jeopardized the line of the promised offspring because of his fear, so Judah's fear did the same in this instance. In each case, God preserved the family line through the "righteousness" of a Gentile—Abimelech and Tamar (see 20:4; 38:26). Interestingly, the book of Ruth also parallels the story of Tamar with the preservation of the line of Judah by the Gentile Ruth (see Ruth 4:12–21).

Tamar's words did more than save her life, preserve the line, and expose Judah's sin. Unbeknownst to her, they also cued the spotlight to shine on the elephant in the room that had followed Judah from Hebron. "Please examine and see," Tamar said. Judah and his brothers had used the same words—identical in the Hebrew text—to get their father to identify Joseph's bloodstained coat. Just compare Genesis 37:32 and 38:25.

As Tamar gave birth to Judah's sons, the "younger" of the twins shoved his way out of the womb first. This would have reminded Judah that God still often works with the older brother serving the younger—just as Joseph's dreams had shown.

So as we return to Joseph's story in Genesis 39, we realize we never really left it. Neither had Judah, though he had tried. And even though there's a gap that veils the other brothers' stories during this time, we don't have to know what happened to each of them in order to know what happened to all of them: God refused to let any of them forget Joseph.

The years passed. But their guilty consciences would not.

Genesis 39 begins with the same information that ended chapter 37. An Egyptian officer named Potiphar, the captain of Pharaoh's bodyguard, bought Joseph from the Ishmaelites (see 39:1).

This seventeen-year-old boy entered Egypt isolated, bewildered, and forsaken. Alone, yet not alone: "The LORD was with Joseph, so he became a successful man" (v. 2). This one verse summarizes what happened in the Egyptian gap between Joseph as a "youth" and a "man." More importantly, it tells us *why* it happened. Joseph became successful because the Lord was with him. We aren't told exactly how many years this represented.

God caused all Joseph did to prosper, and Potiphar noticed. As a result, he promoted Joseph to become his personal servant—responsible for everything in his household. And all that Joseph touched flourished.

But Potiphar wasn't the only one who noticed Joseph. "Now Joseph was handsome in form and appearance. It came about after these events that his master's wife looked with desire at Joseph" (vv. 6–7). It's worth noting that Joseph's handsome frame wasn't all that caught Mrs. Potiphar's eye. She looked at him "after these events." What events? Potiphar gave more and more household duties to Joseph so that, eventually, Potiphar "did not concern himself with anything except the food which he ate" (v. 6). He was never home during the day. Why should he be? Joseph took care of everything. All Potiphar did at home was show up to eat. It's hard to keep a marriage healthy on that kind of interaction. She lost respect for her husband (her words later affirm this).

Joseph, on the other hand, was respectful, responsible, attentive, successful, good looking—and *available*.

Her proposition was anything but subtle. Brazen and bold, she knew how a man's mind works. No small talk, no winks across the room, just straight to business.

"Lie with me," she said.

We read that in English. Moses wrote it in Hebrew. She spoke it in Egyptian. But I'd call that direct in any language.

Pretend for a moment you don't know Joseph's response. Think instead of the situation he finds himself in at this moment. His brothers have severed the family connection; he's a lonely stranger in a strange land; he has zero spiritual encouragement (or accountability); he's a slave with few pleasures in life, if any. On top of that, God revealed to Joseph he would rule over his family. But that clearly wasn't happening. ("Let's see what will happen to his dreams now!") Looking at the circumstances, Joseph was free and clear of his past. Oh, and remember who Potiphar was—the captain of Pharaoh's bodyguard. That means when it came time to pick a wife, he probably didn't make his selection from the leftover spinsters. He would have selected Miss Egypt 1900 BC. The temptation came from a beautiful woman.

Joseph was a red-blooded young man with normal desires, and this stunning woman just handed him a tray of fried pies with an ice-cold glass of milk.

But in the same way that her proposition was straightforward, so also was Joseph's response.

> But he refused and said to his master's wife, "Behold, with me here, my master does not concern himself with anything in the house, and he has put all that he owns in my charge. There is no

one greater in this house than I, and he has withheld nothing from me except you, because you are his wife. How then could I do this great evil and sin against God?" (vv. 8–9)

His immediate reaction was not to say how flattered he was, or to express that "maybe under other circumstances things might be different," or in any way to beat around the bush by way of conversation.

He flatly refused her.

He also told her why. He had a responsibility to his master (and she did too), but more importantly, he had accountability to God (implying, again, that so did she). Joseph branded her suggested fling as a "great evil" that amounted to "sin against God."

He saw the act through God's eyes, not his own.

These are the first words we hear from Joseph in Egypt, and frankly they bring us some relief. In spite of all that has transpired, we see clearly what we may have wondered before now. Joseph still refused to abandon God. Instead, he refused to comply with her evil invitation. Neither had he abandoned his masculinity or even his sexuality. He simply understood God's proper context for it.

And this wasn't it.

God is no prude. He invented sex. In fact, the Bible clearly reveals that a desire to experience sex is natural, normal, and even blessed by God. It would be unrealistic and unbiblical to suggest otherwise. There's nothing unspiritual about being sexual.

The Song of Solomon expresses it well: "Let his left hand be under my head and his right hand embrace me. I adjure you, O daughters of Jerusalem, by the gazelles or by the hinds of the field, that you do not arouse or awaken my love until she pleases" (Song of Sol. 2:6–7). The words *arouse* and *awaken* stem from the same root word in the Hebrew language, a term that means "to arouse to activity as if to awaken someone from sleep." The original wording offers deeper nuances than the English. *Arouse* means one causes it or makes it happen, and *awaken* reflects an intensity, or a repetition, as if overemphasizing its beginning. This woman feels a God-given sexual desire for her fiancé but understands that God intends the desire to be expressed in a proper context. She's urging other young women to wait and not *arouse* that desire until it's the right time. Nor should they be so enamored and obsessed with sex that it's all they think about. There's nothing wrong with the desire. The problem comes by fanning the flame outside the proper context.

But notice the helpful word in this woman's counsel: *until*. That word reminds us we don't have to wait forever. God has a context in which he blesses sex. Joseph knew to wait for it.

Where did Joseph get the wisdom to wait on God versus grabbing what seemed expedient? He had no book of Genesis to read. Joseph *was* Genesis! But he had oral tradition as good as Scripture that served as God's Word before Moses began to write it down. Joseph may have remembered Abraham and Sarah's impatient decision to impregnate Hagar, or Esau's impetuous swap of ready-made stew for his birthright, or Reuben's impulsive one-night stand with his stepmother in hopes of jumping the claim to leadership.

Each of these failures—and more we could list—represented a refusal to wait on God. Joseph knew of them all. He chose to wait.

Avoiding the temptation to compromise one's purity requires more than a onetime decision. As Joseph discovered, it demands a ruthless, daily, moment-by-moment commitment. Potiphar's wife persistently pursued Joseph as the forbidden fruit: "As she spoke to Joseph day after day, he did not listen to her to lie beside her or be with her" (Gen. 39:10). Joseph had said no with his mind long before he said no with his words. He predetermined—day after day—he would live a pure life. He established patterns of behavior that assisted him to succeed, refusing to listen to her or even to be in her company. Why? Because continued exposure to immorality can wear down one's determination to stay pure, and the everyday presence of someone of the opposite sex can trigger a familiarity that opens the door for compromise.

One night just before bed I thumbed a quick email reminder to myself on my smartphone. The autocorrect feature replaced my sloppy typing of "thots" in the subject line with what it assumed I meant. I hit "send" without proofing the email. The next day, as I checked my inbox, I was shocked to see a vulgar word for women's breasts as the subject line of my email to myself! Good grief. Sometimes technology does us no favors! (At times I've roared with laughter, and in other moments stood shocked, at what autocorrect thought I meant.) Later, I thought about the fact that my smartphone may have pulled back the curtain on the "thots" of many of us men—if not most of us. It's a battle. But those of us committed to walking with Christ also stay committed to taking every thought captive.

Most of us, both men and women, if directly propositioned as Joseph was, would refuse just as he did. We'd spot the obvious trap. The tougher temptation comes from the "day after day"—the drip, drip, drip of temptation—an erosion of our resolve by the constant barrage from a sensual world. Knowing it's there for the taking any time we want it. All we have to do is say yes. The constant drip, drip, drip also requires constant vigilance, keeping our thoughts guarded. The problem is not just from the outside.

As Judah discovered, the sex drive can pull at our will like a rare earth magnet. Give the magnet plenty of space, away from a metal, and the attraction is minimal. But if we toy with temptation and scoot the magnet a little closer, then a little closer, one day without warning the two objects will begin a collision course of attraction—and there's no going back.

The problem is not with the magnetic quality of the sex drive. That's of God. The problem comes in ignoring wisdom's call to keep the objects apart until the context is appropriate. Wisdom knows to keep the distance. Fools walk the line.

Solomon asked, "Can a man scoop fire into his lap without his clothes being burned? Can a man walk on hot coals without his feet being scorched? So is he who sleeps with another man's wife; no one who touches her will go unpunished" (Prov. 6:27–29 NIV). A fire in the fireplace is a great thing. It warms the house and provides a relaxing ambiance. But when a spark pops out onto the carpet, we immediately smother it—or it can burn down the whole house.

Joseph made the decision he did because he knew he had a master on earth and a God in heaven, both of whom would hold him accountable. I like how the apostle Paul, while under house arrest in Rome, referred to himself as a "prisoner of Christ Jesus" (Eph. 3:1; Philem. 1, 9). As God's servants, we must decide ahead of time how we will refuse sin when the magnetism starts tugging and when that spark hits the rug. God programmed the sex drive to respond to triggers. Unless we hinder the progression, step one leads to step two, and step two leads to step three—and so on. If we don't choose how we'll respond to temptation, we will react to it instead—and that's frightening.

I'll never forget a day I experienced this.

I traveled with some missionaries to Moscow to help train national pastors. On our first morning, I headed to the hotel lobby to meet our team. Stepping out of the elevator, I scanned the lobby for others in our group. I saw no one I knew.

A small group of ladies at the bar sat and chatted with each other—all of them, that is, except one.

This one very attractive woman was smiling and staring—straight at me. At first I thought she was looking at someone else. Then I remembered someone had told me that prostitutes sat in the bar, trolling for customers. This woman kept smiling and then leaned toward me. As our eyes met, a literal chill ran up my back. I can still feel it. I froze.

At that moment, three very distinct words darted into my head. Only three words. But they were freighted with meaning.

My son, run!

Those three words came from two verses I had learned years earlier. "My son" came from the book of Proverbs, which uses the phrase twenty-three times. But I knew which of those verses God meant for me: "My son . . . Do not desire her beauty in your heart, nor let her capture you with her eyelids. For on account of a harlot one is reduced to a loaf of bread, and an adulteress hunts for the precious life" (Prov. 6:20, 25–26). The word *run* jerked my mind to the other side of the Bible, where Paul warned fellow believers, "Flee from sexual immorality. All other sins a man commits are outside his body, but he who sins sexually sins against his own body" (1 Cor. 6:18 NIV).

Believe it or not, all this ran through my brain in about two seconds as I heard, *My son, run!*

As this woman leered at me, my eyes widened and adrenaline shot through my body. I backed up like a rodeo horse, without even turning around, right into an open elevator—and the doors closed in front of my eyes!

Have you ever almost stepped out into a busy intersection and gotten run over? That's how I felt at that moment. My heart raced like a captive bird. The incident scared me to death. I believe the Holy Spirit brought those verses to my mind. I simply had put that truth in my memory years earlier, and the Lord pointed me to it in the moment I needed it. (As well as to the elevator.)

Joseph's final day in Potiphar's house had a nearly identical application.

Day after day, Mrs. Potiphar harassed Joseph with her flirtations. Because the handsome Hebrew had refused to be with her, even casually, she had to get the jump on him—literally—and surprise him.

Her strategy for seducing Joseph betrayed a growing desperation. First she eyed him, then she spoke to him, then she badgered him, and finally she grabbed him by his clothes and insisted, "Lie with me!" Because she knew they were alone in the house at the moment of her desperate grab, I doubt she wore a formal evening gown. Her clothing was likely as provocative as her proposal.

Adrenaline shot through Joseph's body, and he showed no hesitation: "He left his garment in her hand and fled, and went outside" (Gen. 39:12). Joseph illustrates a principle the rest of the Bible expresses without stuttering. In the war against sexual temptation, Scripture consistently commands one course of action: *flee* (see Song of Sol. 2:7; 1 Cor. 6:18; 2 Tim. 2:22).

Never stand toe-to-toe against sexual temptation. That's too close. Your rare earth magnet will snap together in a fatal attraction. Don't try to analyze how safe you are. God's Word has already done that for you and gives you a simple, understandable command: run for your life! Or perhaps we could say for *the sake of* your life. With sexual temptation, you face a threat that will not only rob your innocence but also rape your mind with memories you'll regret for the rest of your life—God's forgiveness notwithstanding. Ask anybody you know who has crossed the line. It's never worth it.

Yet our fleeing is not flailing—it is a resolute focus, like that of a sprinter headed for the tape. That's because we do more than merely run *from* something in any direction; we also run *to* something. Paul wrote, "Flee from youthful lusts and pursue righteousness" (2 Tim. 2:22). We could look at it this way: we flee lusts *by* pursuing righteousness. We do both at the same time.

For Joseph, he determined neither to listen to her nor to be with her. And when the situation called for it, he even ran from her. He faced each day with a plan he would follow when tempted. We need the same strategy.

We need to take a sober look at our consistent temptations and predetermine how we'll respond the next time we face them. Because we will. Perhaps we have a verse we can quote. Maybe we have an accountability partner to call or text. For sure we need to decide that—no matter what—we're going to run. No matter what we lose. No matter what the cost. Joseph left some of his clothes. We may have to leave much more. Our job. Our pride. An investment. Just name it. What's our integrity worth?

Personally, I find it helpful to choose ahead of time that my impulsive reaction will be *immediate obedience*. Whenever I feel a pang of temptation and see a fried pie, I immediately force my eyes to move, and more importantly, I force my heart to move. Like pulling someone from the edge of a cliff, I try to be that instantaneous and fierce in my determination. I love the words of the old Puritan John Owen in his helpful book *The Mortification of Sin*:

> Rise mightily against the first actings of thy distemper, its first conceptions; suffer it not to get the least ground. Do not say, "Thus far it shall go and no farther." If it have allowance for one step it will take another. It is impossible to fix bounds to sin. It is like water in a channel—if it once break out, it will have its course. Its not acting is easier to be compassed than its bounding.[1]

Have you ever ridden a horse that wanted to run for the barn? You have to keep constant tension on the reins and never for one moment relax your grip. For some horses, you have to keep them from even *seeing* the barn. If you neglect to control your mount, and that animal begins to trot barn-ward, you will find yourself riding an animal out of control.

The secret to handling the horse in our hearts comes from keeping a tight rein on our sinful nature. Never give it an inch of slack. As docile as it promises to be, as tame as it has proven itself over the years, never trust it. It will betray you if you let it.

But there's another part of our hearts that isn't so glandular or instinctive. Its motivations find their passion and absolute delight in everything that is God. This part of our lives comes from the Spirit of God who lives within us, blessing us with the natural outworking of his nature. When we surrender to his control, we find our lives portraying his character of love, joy, peace, patience, kindness, goodness, faithfulness, and—perhaps most essential in the context of sexual temptation—self-control.

These two natures within the Christian are diametrically opposed to each other and will never shake hands. One is a magnet; the other is a commitment. One is a reaction; the other is a decision. One is immediate but temporary; the other is delayed and eternal. One makes our hearts long for the here and now; the other makes our hearts ache for the next life. This tension is summarized well by Paul's question: "Wretched man that I am! Who will set me free from the body of this death?" (Rom. 7:24). The tension only ends when life does and we go home to Jesus.

Interestingly, the strongest argument for sexual purity is not the threat of disease, pregnancy, or public shame. The reason we choose purity comes from the reality of who owns our lives (see 1 Cor. 6:15–20). That was Joseph's appeal.

We are not our own. We were "bought with a price," body and soul (v. 20).

When Potiphar's wife grabbed Joseph, he didn't pray about what to do. He didn't share the four spiritual laws with her. He didn't even repeat the words he had spoken earlier. He simply twisted out of the clothes she clutched and fled. Then the text notes, oddly, "she left his garment [literally 'to lie'] beside her until his master came home" (Gen. 39:16).

The oddity of that phrase causes our ears to perk up.

And it should. Here's why.

4

Going Backward,
Moving Forward

He was there in the jail. But the Lord was with Joseph and extended kindness to him.

Genesis 39:20–21

As the adage goes, "Hell hath no fury like a woman scorned." As soon as Joseph escaped and left Mrs. Potiphar holding nothing but his clothes, she shouted for the household servants and concocted a story that the Hebrew came inside with the intent to rape her, but she screamed and he ran outside.

How noble. How moral. *How unusual*, the servants must have thought.

Her response, however, betrayed the real object of her fury—which wasn't Joseph. She blamed Potiphar for the problem, both to the servants and then to his face (see Gen. 39:13–18). Again, we get a window into their relationship.

No one witnessed the scene, of course. The incident transpired behind closed doors. So who will Potiphar believe—his wife or his slave? The one he has to live with or the one easily disposed of? The Egyptian wife or the Hebrew patsy? Sadly, the same thing often happens today as did then. The one with the power wins. When Potiphar heard the story, he fumed and chose to incarcerate Joseph (see v. 20).

This is pure conjecture on my part, but I'm not convinced Potiphar believed his wife—even though Joseph got the guilty verdict. For starters, any other slave who attempted to rape his wife would likely have lost his head. But Potiphar knew Joseph's character as well as the character of his accuser. And remember, she had just falsely accused Potiphar too. I think Potiphar put Joseph in jail to save face—as well as to keep a good servant. Who knows, maybe he also did it to save Joseph's life. Mrs. Potiphar may have demanded Joseph's death in order to keep him from spilling the beans. All pure conjecture, I admit—but all possible.

I recently completed listening to the whole Bible in a year while commuting to work each day. It took longer to listen to it than to read it, of course, but the experience helped me connect with the Word of God in a way much closer to the way the original recipients interacted with Scripture—by hearing it. In the days before the printing press, a common believer would not have had any personal copies of the Bible (the average American home today has five). Biblical authors originally wrote to a *listening* audience—to hearers, not readers.

When Moses wrote down Joseph's story, the old man committed to parchment what had existed previously only as oral tradition. The Spirit of God inspired Moses to record without error thousands of years of oral history in the book of Genesis. The late David Dorsey wrote a wonderful book called *The Literary Structure of the Old Testament*, in which he notes:

> The blandness of an ancient text's appearance reflects the cultural reality that ancient texts were written primarily to be heard, not seen. . . . Signals were geared for the ear, not the eye, since visual markers would be of little value to a listening audience. . . . Ancient Hebrew structuring patterns and techniques were different from ours. . . . These and related patterns are so foreign to modern readers that it is easy to miss—or misunderstand—them.[1]

I bring this up to highlight something we can miss by merely reading the English Bible. The Hebrew text gives signals to the ear, words or phrases that connect one part of a story with another. We've already mentioned a couple of them, like the line "Please examine and see," spoken by both Joseph's brothers and Tamar.

But another connection is far more understated—and offers tremendous insights. Hebrew texts sometimes communicate emphasis by way of structure. For example, in English, we have poetry whose lines we label as A, B, C, D, and then the concepts, words, or rhyme schemes repeat in reverse—D', C', B', A'. If we look at these lines arranged graphically, they appear visually as an X, equivalent to the Greek letter X or *chi*. For this reason, this type of structure is called a *chiasm* (or *chiasmus*). The Hebrew hearers understood when they perceived this type of structure that the author was emphasizing the center of the chiasm.

Don't worry, this isn't Bible code or some Kabbalah nonsense or a "secret" cipher. It's just that the Bible originally had a listening audience, with audible connections inspired into the text to aid in memory, understanding, and application. The acrostic of Psalm 119 is another, more familiar, example of a memory device.

Thousands of chiasms appear in the Hebrew text, and we find some significant ones in Joseph's story. Most notably, as the account of Joseph's temptation by Potiphar's wife unfolds, the chiasm spotlights the point in the story when she kept Joseph's garment to "*lie* beside her." Why would that odd phrase prove so significant? Because the previous story's chiasm climaxed when Judah *lay* with Tamar.

The two emphases stand as a stark contrast. They arrest our attention for good reasons.

Both Judah and Joseph have left home to live for an extended time in another culture. Both have suffered loss without consolation. Neither has any godly influence or accountability. In the midst of these vulnerable moments, each man faced temptation by a woman who offered illicit and secret intercourse. Both brothers had an immediate response.

Judah sought solace for his grief and relief for his sensual pangs through the exhilaration of forbidden fruit. Growing up in a family context of "take what you want," Judah did just that. Judah used sex as a sedative to a disappointing life. Potiphar's wife tried to do the same. And frankly, so do many people today—through alcohol, or relationships, or food, or work, or busyness, or ministry, or, or, or . . . all substitutes for a life without a firm foundation on God.

Of course, some of these alternatives look nobler than others. Some will even win awards. But at their root lies an oblivious motivation of idolatry. Like my ignorant episode with the fried pies, many people tired of waiting on God try to alleviate their pain by eating the very thing that's causing it. "No one can live without delight," Thomas Aquinas observed, "and that is why a man deprived of spiritual joy goes over to carnal pleasures."[2]

The lure of temptation itches like poison ivy. It screams for scratching, as if satisfaction can come no other way. But in reality, scratching only makes the itch worse. True satisfaction comes by refusing to scratch and allowing God's process of healing and health to take its course.

It may seem strange that God would create us as physical beings with appetites, inclinations, and passions for hunger and sex and work but then also command us at times to flat-out refuse these yearnings. No wonder the world sees us as oddballs!

But God also created us as spiritual beings, and the two parts of our natures remain inseparably intertwined. One affects the other. That's why Joseph's denial of Potiphar's wife was not a denial of his sexuality. It was, in fact, an affirmation of it. His spiritual life worked in concert with his physical one.

At a point of temptation and extreme physical hunger, Jesus said, "Man shall not live on bread alone, but on every word that proceeds out of the mouth of God" (Matt. 4:4). Jesus reminded the tempter that God never designed people to live merely as physical beings. Rather, our physical decisions always go hand in hand with our spiritual lives. Our bodies are temples of the Holy Spirit, and any decision that compromises our walk with God can never be God's will for our bodies—however great the pangs seem to scream. "Thou hast made us for Thyself," Augustine observed, "and our hearts are restless till they find rest in Thee."³ Until we put God at the center of our significance, our loneliness, our sexuality, and our purpose, we will never get satisfaction—only a temporary gratification that intensifies our pain.

Just because Joseph remained faithful doesn't mean his temptation proved any easier than Judah's. Joseph grew up in the same family, but he chose a different path. God's grace opened Joseph's eyes to the bigger results of self-gratification. He made a conscious determination *not* to gratify himself, because he understood that, even if no one else would see, God would. Joseph's perspective saw the pleasure of sex as an act within the broader context of walking with God—a physical expression of the spiritual life.

Joseph chose to wait for God's timing for sexual expression—if it even came at all. To do otherwise amounted to sin against God.

When expectations about what life "ought to be" go unmet for extended periods of time, our hearts will want to drift into fantasy. Longstanding bouts with tough circumstances—a debilitating illness, family issues, sexual frustration, money problems, marital struggles, and general discontent—offer the greatest temptations to fantasize how great it would be to live in other "ideal" circumstances.

We'll see some other person's life and imagine that if *we* had what *they* have, then we wouldn't feel the way we do. If we only lived there, not here, then we would be a different person. *If my father would only . . . if my spouse would finally . . . if God would simply . . . then all would be well.*

This thinking is bunk.

We are not the victims of life we think we are. We are sinners God has chosen by grace to mold into his image. Hasn't the Lord promised to care for our needs? And if he chooses to wait to do so, and to cause us to wait to receive them, might he have a reason?

Because he is God, he has the prerogative to determine what's best for us—including keeping from us what we really, really want—if he deems it wise.

Fantasy, on the other hand, dwells on lies. With very few exceptions, tough circumstances simply reveal the holes in our hearts, not the holes in our lives. Situations only reveal the areas where we need to grow. The problem isn't our meager circumstance as much as it is our hearts' refusal to trust in God's sovereignty. Fantasy is a longing to be out of the will of God. When we imagine another reality for ourselves, we set our minds on our interests and not on God's. (As if we could ever imagine a reality that's better for us than God can.)

When we find ourselves feeling marooned on Fantasy Island with no way off, we need to do all we can to discover the way of obedience. Then we take it, regardless of the cost, and wait there for God.

Though it sounds strange, remember that even Jesus, "although He was a Son . . . learned obedience from the things which He suffered" (Heb. 5:8). Don't get sidetracked with the difficult theology embedded in that verse. The bottom line is that if the Son of God learned obedience through suffering—through betrayal, heartache, temptation, and loneliness—why would it be any different for us? If Jesus, of all people, could not avoid it, we certainly will not.

Even if we *were* in other circumstances, we're still just us. That's the problem. When we chase our fantasy about life somewhere over the rainbow, we discover the yellow brick road only takes us to another dead end in the labyrinth.

We find ourselves still trapped by our real problem—a discontented heart.

Joseph came from a family in which sexual restraint took a backseat to getting what one wanted. Judah's story reminds us of that weakness. But waiting on God for satisfaction is a principle that extends beyond sexuality to our entire walk with God. Although this event in Joseph's life appears to center on sexual temptation, it really focuses on testing Joseph's character.

Every sin we commit represents a failure to wait on God. Try to think of an exception. Sin begins in the mind, where we choose a shortcut to joy, fulfillment, or relief. Our struggle to wait on God for satisfaction often comes because the new life God is leading us toward doesn't seem as great as the one he has redeemed us from. We miss some part of the past.

If we're honest, too many days our words sound like those of the Hebrews who lived after Joseph—those redeemed from slavery and yet unsatisfied with freedom: "We remember the fish which we used to eat free in Egypt, the cucumbers and the melons and the leeks and the onions and the garlic" (Num. 11:5). We all struggle with this kind of discontentment. And in those moments, we betray our selective memories.

When we grumble about the waiting God requires, we're only considering half of the truth. We remember the pleasures of captivity—the leeks, onions, and fish (your menu may be different)—but we forget the bondage God redeemed us from (not to mention that whole lake of fire thing in hell). Our minds focus on all the sensory losses and none of the spiritual benefits. It's never the lack of spiritual connection with God we remember from the past. It's the pleasure of sin's shortcuts to immediate gratification. Never mind that we cried out to the Lord to deliver us from our guilt. Forget that we had no hope for the future. All things being equal, we prefer leeks to manna. What we had seems better than what we have.

When God removes something from our lives—something we had in abundance years ago—a number of emotional triggers kick in. Like being angry with God, or being tempted to sin, or coveting someone else's life. Happiness becomes our top priority. We want to take what looks good without thought of the consequences—like David, who for his one-night stand with Bathsheba endured a lifelong, agonizing sword that never departed from his family (see 2 Sam. 12:9–10). We think we should get more for our hard work, like Gehazi, who connived to get money that wasn't his to take and therefore lived out his days as a leper (see 2 Kings 5:20–27).

We remember the zing of immediate gratification we got apart from God, but we forget the painful bondage from which we cried to him for deliverance. We crave the best of two incompatible worlds.

Like Judah, in moments of unguarded passion, we'll hand over our seal and cord—our purity, our financial security, or our integrity—thinking that anything is worth what we'll gain in this moment. We want to give our mind, ego, and reputation what God refuses to give them. We have waited for years for the Lord to improve our situation with no hope it will ever change. The lack of results screams to us to sidestep our values, since waiting on God seems to accomplish nothing. It seems all academic and impractical.

In the courts of human opinion, it seems God plays unfair. He fails to keep his promises when we define his faithfulness in terms of our ideal life. Our problem? We only have human brains. Limited. Shortsighted. Impatient. Self-focused. We set up the standards by which God should rule the world, and then we crucify him when he lets us down.

When God fails to open the door for us to enter our ideal life, it's tempting just to chase it ourselves. We'll issue God an ultimatum, and if he misses the deadline we'll assume he approves. We begin to make decisions based on feelings of entitlement—as if we've waited long enough. We deserve to move ahead. It's time. God is welcome to follow as an optional guest.

I heard a radio ad that began, "They say good things come to those who wait. But who wants to wait?" The marketer played into the weakness of human nature by goading our impatience with the needlessness of waiting. It's an old tactic.

We have to remember that Satan is the best marketer in the sin business. He can stretch a thin veil of splendor over a heap of dung and convince us to buy it. The devil uses the pleasures of sin as a down payment, because he knows he gets back double for his investment. He loses nothing; we lose a lot. In those moments when the old life seems better than the new, when complaining replaces gratitude, when immediate gratification appeals more than delayed satisfaction, we need to put our brains in neutral and survey the full picture.

Our enemy is invisible, deceitful, and bent on our destruction. The one who tells us there's no need to wait wants to hurry our demise. The Word of God isn't a series of rules to prohibit freedom but a divine guide to provide victory over that which would kill.

Every obedient act is a victory—whether or not we see the results on this side of eternity. Although our mistakes will never thwart God's sovereign plan, they certainly can affect our privileged participation in it—as well as potential blessings God would have given (see 2 Sam. 12:8).

But forget sinful longings for a moment. Even when our hunger in life is only for the good things God withholds, the same lesson applies. Discontentment about God's meager provision comes from a failure to see the value of God's will.

When the apostle Paul penned, "Love is patient" (1 Cor. 13:4), he literally wrote, "Love is *being patient*." The original Greek word means that patience is a continual decision we make. So why do we so often choose impatience? The next verse tells us love "does not seek its own" (v. 5). Impatience grows from the root of selfishness. We want what we want—and right *now*, please.

Selfishness refuses to wait on God or trust God to lead in his time. Selfishness wants God to act immediately. But do we really? If we knew what God knows, we would choose to wait for his timing.

Waiting on God seems passive. It feels like we're sitting in the ash heap with poor Job, scraping ourselves with the shards of our broken life.

On the contrary, waiting is a very active part of living. Waiting on God, if we do it correctly, is anything but passive. Waiting works its way out in very deliberate actions, very intentionally searching the Scriptures and praying, intense moments of humility, and self-realization of our finiteness. With the waiting comes learning. I can't think of much I've learned that's positive from the times I've plowed ahead without waiting on God.

God made his creatures to live in dependence on their Creator. As such, we wait for the provision he gives "in due time" (Ps. 145:15). Dependence demands waiting. Refusing to wait amounts to independence and even rebellion against the one who created us. Insisting on instant gratification, even for good things, minimizes and overlooks the infinite worth of God's sovereignty—a wisdom that sees beyond the next five minutes. Or the next five years.

It is necessary, therefore, for us to remain in God's moral will while we wait on him. Otherwise, how will we recognize his voice if we have, through impatience, wandered out of the bounds of truth? Even if we *were* to hear from God during this time—when he finally leads us—we wouldn't have confidence in his leading. Scripture reveals that a commitment to a renewed mind is precursory to recognizing "his good, pleasing and perfect will" (Rom. 12:2 NIV). If we abandon that part of his moral will of which we're certain, we will have little confidence of his leading in the uncertain direction of our future. Our faithfulness to God must find its motivation in our resolve, not in its results.

God often keeps quiet about why he allows what he allows in our lives. Although God can handle all of our questions, we cannot handle all of his answers. As with Job, if God *did* answer our complaints, we would only put our hands over our mouths at our embarrassing inability to grasp the mind of God (see Job 40:4). To paraphrase Jack Nicholson, "We can't handle the truth!" Only eternity will reveal how often God's best answer to us was to say nothing.

However, he does promise his presence—a need far greater than we can comprehend. Although we lack understanding, we do know that *he* understands, and that's enough—because he is with us.

Whatever God removes from us, he has not removed himself. He never will.

That's why we need to notice that all of these events in Joseph's life occurred while "the LORD was with Joseph" (Gen. 39:2, 21). God was with Joseph when Mrs. Potiphar flirted with him. The Lord stood by his side when she made her lewd come-ons. And the Almighty held Joseph's hand as he fled for his life.

Yes, God was with Joseph. Yet Joseph's integrity didn't instantly vindicate him. It seems Joseph's faithfulness earned him nothing but a false accusation and wrongful imprisonment. But it turned out to be much more than that.

It was an answer to prayer.

Day after day, Joseph endured the lurid glances, the immoral flirting, and finally the physical harassment. Although the Bible keeps silent on how many days or months Joseph endured the drip, drip, drip of her seductive invitations, we can be certain Joseph, a man of God, cried out to the Lord for deliverance and pleaded for help in this time of relentless testing.

Finally, deliverance came in an unusual way: Joseph went to jail.

Joseph probably never thought the answer to his prayer for deliverance would take him to prison. In a way, this must have seemed like déjà vu for Joseph. Just as his wrongful betrayal by his brothers freed him from the influence of his dysfunctional family, so his wrongful imprisonment via Potiphar's wife unfettered him from her daily temptations.

He was imprisoned—but in truth Joseph was freer than he had been in a long time.

God used the unfair situations and accusations to advance the plan he had revealed to Joseph in his dreams. Rather than regressing, God's plan for Joseph was progressing. Did Joseph understand how? No way. Neither do we. That's why what happened next affirmed to Joseph what we also need to remember in our lives:

> But the LORD was with Joseph and extended kindness to him, and gave him favor in the sight of the chief jailer. . . . The chief jailer did not supervise anything under Joseph's charge because the LORD was with him; and whatever he did, the LORD made to prosper. (Gen. 39:21, 23)

Sounds familiar, doesn't it? The inspired text intends we see these events, however confusing, as coming from God's hand.

Once again, repeated cues help us make the connections. It seemed like someone was always tearing off Joseph's coat. Whether it was his brothers stripping him of the coat of many colors or Mrs. Potiphar ripping off his garment, in both instances the clothes served as evidence to fabricate a lie about him. In both cases, he was lied about by the guilty ones who produced the clothing. In both cases, he went from a place of prominence to a pit—and then back to a place of prominence.

In every pit Joseph got dropped into, the Lord caused him to rise to the top of the heap. The hard transitions in life came from God's sovereign plan, not simply from the cruelties of people.

Joseph's demotions were God's sovereign promotions.

Think about that in your life as well. If you pray, as Jesus taught us, for God to "lead us not into temptation, but deliver us from evil," and your situation seems to get worse, it may be God's way of answering your prayer and intervening in a way so wise you simply cannot fathom the path.

All the more reason to abandon the fantasies and to dig in with faithfulness wherever God puts us. Often we'll discover the progression of God's will in our lives occurs by him taking us two steps back to go three steps forward.

Those two steps back are the gaps in which we find ourselves waiting on God. They're the red lights with no cross traffic. They're the seasons of life when we feel imprisoned, forgotten, idle, and forsaken.

"But the LORD was with Joseph." And he is with us too. So we wait on him.

What happens next to Joseph shows us how to do it.

Part II

LETTING GO

5

CIRCLING IN THE ROUND HOUSE

They afflicted his feet with fetters,
He himself was laid in irons;
Until the time that his word came to pass,
The word of the LORD *tested him.*

Psalm 105:18–19

My first high school had round buildings with pie-shaped classrooms. The hallways circled the perimeters of the buildings. The campus looked as if spaceships had landed in San Antonio. Students from rival high schools referred to us as "the round school for squares." Nice, huh?

For fun, we would pull a prank on new students who asked for directions to a classroom: "Yeah, just walk down the hall and turn left at the corner." They would circle for hours.

Sometimes our walk with God feels like we're the butt of some such juvenile prank. He points the direction, and we walk and walk and walk. But we never turn a corner. We follow but go nowhere.

We walk, and yet, we wait. God's goal for leading us, it seems, isn't to take us somewhere as much as it is for us to follow. Whether we walk or run on this treadmill of God's will, we still seem to make no progress. Nevertheless, the process gets us in shape.

Falsely accused and unfairly convicted, Joseph found himself jailed in the house of the captain of the bodyguard. The Hebrew text literally refers to the jail as the "house of roundness," or "the Round House," perhaps the name of the prison-fortress (see Gen. 39:20). As Joseph began to circle in the Round House in the months that followed his imprisonment, he may have felt like the victim of a juvenile prank. And yet, the Bible affirms, "the LORD was with Joseph," a phrase that appears four times, twice after his cruel sale into slavery and twice again after his unjust confinement in prison (see 39:2–3, 21, 23). We can't escape the truth of that statement.

God lay behind everything Joseph experienced.

Although Genesis keeps a tight lip on the exact length of time Joseph spent circling in the Round House, we do know his time in Egypt totaled eleven years so far (see 37:2; 41:1, 46). He likely served at least one year in Potiphar's house—for it would take time for God's blessing to show itself "in the field" (39:5). The majority of these years seems to have been in the jail where he was "bound"— the literal meaning in Hebrew for "imprisoned" (40:3). Psalm 105 confirms this and adds something Genesis doesn't mention:

> They afflicted his feet with fetters,
> He himself was laid in irons;
> Until the time that his word came to pass,
> The word of the LORD tested him. (vv. 18–19)

Joseph's imprisonment included fetters on his ankles and an iron collar around his neck. Imagine the everyday reality of those encumbering conditions. Each night as he slept, the collar pressed against his throat. Every time he used the restroom, he had to maneuver around the manacles. With each movement he made or step he took, the chains rattled and clanked. Moreover, the fetters "afflicted" his feet—a term in Hebrew that includes humiliation as well as pain.

The text portrays the place he found himself imprisoned as miserable. Part of his struggle came from the monotony, the mundane routine, the same faces, the same four walls—the abysmal lack of variety. Add to all that Joseph's innocence, and he had a tough load to bear.

This was Joseph's life—*for years.*

But the fetters and the collar must have seemed small potatoes compared to the greatest affliction of his imprisonment.

The waiting.

Joseph could count the links in his chains, but he had no idea the number of days he would have to wait on God for the fulfillment of his dreams. During those long, monotonous years of circling in the Round House, God had a purpose for Joseph. Only in Psalm 105:18–19 do we see God's reason for the delay: "He himself was laid in irons; until the time that his word came to pass, the word of the LORD tested him." The words "he himself" are literally "his soul," from a Hebrew word that refers to the whole person. More than Joseph's feet and neck had chains. In context, the shackles confined *all* of who he was—his entire life was on hold, confined in God's waiting room with bars.

God tested Joseph "until the time that *his word* came to pass." The psalmist mentions Joseph's "word," his *dreams,* as the fulcrum of God's testing. Wearing chains would have reminded Joseph of the first time he had been bound—when his brothers betrayed him. Joseph would later refer to the prison as a "dungeon" (Gen. 40:15), literally a "pit," the same term used of the cistern where his brothers dropped him. God caused Joseph to remember his brothers so that he would also recall his dreams—God's revelation to him.

Testing Joseph's moral fiber took only a year or so in Potiphar's house. But the tougher assignment stretched many, many years beyond the first. Would this new gap in God's plan for Joseph—this unfair and unreasonable red light—weaken his faith in God's promise? The brothers' statement continues to echo in our heads: "Then let us see what will become of his dreams!"

That's the real issue here.

God "tested" Joseph, a word in the original language that refers to the process of refining silver. Refining takes time. It took years, in fact—"until the time that his word came to pass."

The test for Joseph was waiting on God.

The chief jailer put Joseph in charge of the jail, "because the LORD was with him; and whatever he did, the LORD made to prosper" (39:23). Specifically, Joseph had the responsibility of all the prisoners.

One day Pharaoh's cupbearer and baker became prisoners in the Round House. No one could have anticipated the significance of these men to Joseph's future—nor the accidental encouragement they would offer him as he waited on God.

Somehow these two officials had offended Pharaoh and found themselves confined in the same prison as Joseph (see 40:1–3). The captain of the bodyguard, namely Potiphar, assigned them to Joseph's care. They were in jail "for some time," or as the Hebrew reads literally, "for days" (v. 4). It's easy to pass over those words. The text implies a lengthy stay. Then something happened.

One morning Joseph noticed the two officials seemed gloomy. When he asked them why they had sad faces, they replied, "We have had a dream and there is no one to interpret it" (v. 8). Okay, wait a minute. This scene strikes me as strange for a couple of reasons.

First of all, why would Joseph even *care* that these guys seemed sad? They were prisoners! They had offended Pharaoh. Why shouldn't they be unhappy? Furthermore, when you feel down yourself, you don't ask why others seem sad. Why? Because they might tell you! Then you would only feel worse. No, when you feel down, melancholy's vacuum sucks you inward to focus on all that's wrong with your own lousy life. Although misery loves company, it can't bear someone else's burden in addition to its own. You don't have the time, energy, or desire to reach out in concern to others. It's all about *you* and *your* pain and *your* victimization and *your* sorry lot in life. Hearing about someone else's troubles only makes yours seem heavier. If Joseph had reacted to his undeserved situation with anger turned inward, his depression would have caused him to ignore these sad officials (who were getting what they deserved) and move on to the next prisoner without a word.

But Joseph chose a different path and asked, "Why are your faces so sad today?" (v. 7). That Joseph even questioned them tells us he deliberately chose to live in a good frame of mind. He had enough peace with God to look beyond his own pain and notice the lives of others.

I admit, at first that observation seems like a stretch—like some sugarcoated platitude lifted from a Sunday school flannel graph. But let's keep observing.

Second, if Joseph knew these men well enough to notice they were sad "today," that means a relationship had developed. In all the days they had spent locked up together, I find it remarkable that Joseph had said nothing about his dreams. We the readers know about them as well as about his ability to understand them. But no one in Egypt knew that. In contrast to his impulsive sharing with his family, Joseph has kept his dreams to himself for eleven years. How do we know? Because if his reputation with dreams had become common knowledge, then the two dreamers in the

Round House would have greeted Joseph in the morning with anticipation. Instead, he found two gloomy faces.

For whatever reason, these officials understood their dreams as meaning more than dog dreams. The dreams had significance, but they felt at a loss to unravel the implications. What's worse, "no one" could help them. No wonder they seemed sad.

Their dreams served at least three purposes for Joseph. The first came immediately, another would come in a few days, and another would take two more years to bear fruit. Immediately, the opportunity to interpret these dreams served as a test for Joseph. These are the first dreams Genesis records after Joseph's dreams, which represented revelation from God. Would Joseph still believe God's words after eleven years?

Joseph could have responded with cynicism. "You had dreams? Ha! Trust me, they'll never amount to anything. I had dreams too, but they have never come true. Best forget them."

But we never catch a hint of that in Joseph's remarks. Instead, Joseph's answer gives us insight into what he thought about his own dreams: "Do not interpretations belong to God?" (v. 8). This response reveals Joseph has neither forgotten his dreams nor given up on them. Instead, he has chosen to wait on God to bring them about.

How would God accomplish them? Joseph had no clue. But one truth he did know: interpretations of dreams belong to God.

Joseph refused to give up on his faith. He had passed this test.

With nothing to lose, the cupbearer shared his dream first, and Joseph related the good news the dream revealed. In three days, Pharaoh would restore the cupbearer to his office with a full pardon. And because the cupbearer would have an audience with Pharaoh in a few days, Joseph took the opportunity to make a request:

Keep me in mind when it goes well with you, and please do me a kindness by mentioning me to Pharaoh and get me out of this house. For I was in fact kidnapped from the land of the Hebrews, and even here I have done nothing that they should have put me into the dungeon. (vv. 14–15)

Here, the Bible pulls up the shade and opens a window into Joseph's emotions. Finally, we get to see through the Superman suit to Joseph's heart. Psalm 105 gives us insight into God's purpose in the waiting, but not until these words do we catch a glimpse of Joseph's feelings about his whole ordeal. We see a man who hurts, who misses home, and who longs for justice. In his request to Pharaoh through the cupbearer, we also catch a glimpse of Joseph's prayers to God these many years. He wants to get out of prison and go home where he belongs.

Joseph uses two words for the prison. The general term, "house," is short for "the Round House" used earlier. But he also calls it a "dungeon," or literally "a pit," connecting it to the cistern in the Dothan Valley that started this whole ordeal. Both his kidnapping from a pit and his incarceration in a pit were unjust. And in an unusual moment of personal request, Joseph asks the cupbearer to keep him in mind and mention him to Pharaoh.

For all Joseph knew, God had sent this man into prison in order to get Joseph out. He could be God's answer to Joseph's prayers. Notice though, as Joseph made his appeal, he kept quiet about his own dreams. He has tipped his hand on his ability to interpret, and he has even shared about the injustices he has borne. But about his dreams, mum's the word.

Perhaps Joseph had learned that communicating about them prematurely, to people unready to hear them, could create problems. Maybe he has learned that God would bring about his plans in his time. Either way, Joseph has learned restraint. He knew much more than he told.

If Joseph could indeed tell the truth about the cupbearer's dream, Joseph was also telling the truth about his own innocence. Three more days would prove it.

Waiting on God doesn't prohibit us from taking initiative or trying to change unjust circumstances. We don't merely lie back and mutter, "Oh, I'm just trusting God with this." God gave us brains to think with as well as courts to appeal to and governments to enforce laws. But we also need to remember the limitations of our brains. We can try to pursue the logical and legal path, but we must submit these to sovereignty. God may have something else in mind neither logical nor legal. His mind, after all, takes logic to another level (see Isa. 55:8–9). We see the next ten dominoes that will fall. God sees the next ten million.

After the baker overheard Joseph's favorable interpretation for the cupbearer, the baker told Joseph his dream as well. But his had a different interpretation entirely. In three days, Joseph said, Pharaoh would hang the baker (see Gen. 40:16–19). Obviously, Joseph didn't ask the baker to remember him!

There you have it. Two dreams, two specific and opposite interpretations, both coming to fulfillment on a specific day. What would happen?

The next three days in the Round House must have felt like forever in the minds of the cupbearer, the baker, and even Joseph. Then on day three, right on schedule, the prison door swung open and Pharaoh's two officials discovered Joseph indeed could interpret dreams. For they transpired precisely as he had predicted.

Joseph must have felt elated. Finally, after eleven years as a slave in Egypt, he looked forward to walking free! At last, all would know his innocence and he would have justice. Now he could escape the pit and return to his father. God had heard his prayers. No more injustice. No more chains. No more misery.

No more waiting.

Joseph listened for footsteps in the hours that followed. Every sound turned his head in expectation of those who would un-bolt the prison door and remove his shackles. Every morning, he glanced immediately toward the door. But days turned to weeks—and weeks to months. And months to years.

No one came.

The Bible tells us plainly what Joseph had to figure out by waiting: "The chief cupbearer did not remember Joseph, but forgot him" (v. 23).

Nobody likes to be forgotten.

When someone close to us overlooks our birthday, or our spouse forgets our anniversary, or a friend misses a lunch date, we feel hurt. The day or time that should have highlighted our importance to someone instead underscored our irrelevance. At least we can feel that way.

When people forget us, or fail us, or even forsake us, we're left alone in the ashes of a reality we never expected—and certainly never wanted. In those intense moments of loneliness, confusion, and emotional ache, we ask God for one thing more than anything: relief. We want relief even more than answers.

But when relief is denied us, we begin the difficult journey of resisting the notion that God is a cruel sovereign who toys with our lives. After all, he could stop it all in a moment. Yet he doesn't. It stings when those close to us forget us. But pain goes to the core of our being when the weeks, months, and years go by with no sign that God sees us as significant.

We know God created each of us to do good works for him (see Eph. 2:10). However, God seldom puts us immediately into the place he ultimately desires us to serve. This proved true with Joseph. But he wasn't the only one.

Noah waited one hundred years for the flood. Abraham waited twenty-five years for his promised son. Moses waited eighty years to liberate his people from Egypt. David waited a dozen years before he would rule Israel. Even Jesus, born king of the Jews, would wait more than thirty years before he presented himself to Israel—and *he still waits* to rule as king (see Heb. 1:13).

We can't miss the obvious truth that in every case listed above, as these individuals waited on God, he prepared them for their ultimate purpose by taking them on a journey they would have preferred to avoid (see Matt. 26:39).

We may realize God has gifted us in some way—we may even have a particular vision for how we can serve God with those gifts—and yet, God does nothing to advance the goal. At times, in fact, it even seems like the Lord thwarts his own plans! Remember, God revealed to Joseph he would rule over his family, and yet Joseph struggled as a slave and a prisoner for years. Joseph's story reveals a principle we must transfer to our lives as well: *God's ultimate plans for us include preparation and waiting.*

I like the question Bill Murray's character asked in the movie *Groundhog Day*: "What would you do if you were stuck in one place, and every day was exactly the same and nothing that you did mattered?" When he asked that question, one of his buddies confessed, "That about sums it up for me." Does that sum it up for you? If we're honest, at times we feel no hope that we'll ever move beyond the grind of life into fulfillment. Instead, we feel stuck in our pursuit of futility.

You've probably noticed that very few people attain stardom status in life. That's a good thing. Fame hangs on the thin wire of "What have you done for me lately?" Agents and fans are always looking for the *next* championship, or the *next* bestseller, or the *next* sell-out event. As soon as you quit producing great stuff, you go from rock star to rock bottom. From the national news to the *National Inquirer*. When you slip to "has-been" status, the general public quits admiring your talent and begins gawping at your weight gain, hair loss, and DWIs.

After watching the Super Bowl or the Oscars, I often think of how the world's glory lasts but a moment. Nobody remembers who won best actor in 1983. Nobody remembers because nobody cares. Worldly success is fickle and fleeting—a siren's song that promises satisfaction but delivers an empty box.

That's why, frankly, I'm glad God made me average and not exceedingly gifted. Oh sure, I'm *pretty* good at several things, but I'm not *great* at anything. And honestly, I'm grateful. Because sometimes we can mistake talent and giftedness as God's call—come hell or high water. I do believe a gift represents a responsibility, especially a spiritual gift. But God gives talents and gifts not for us as individuals but for the edification of the church and for his glory. The goal of any gift is to edify others, not to inflate the ego of the gifted. Joy comes in serving God with our gifts. Otherwise it's fickle fame. An empty box.

We can mistake God's gift for God's will when it comes down to choosing between the exercise of the gift or the focus on a priority more important to God. For example, I know of individuals—some in history and some personally—who were very gifted. *Exceptionally gifted.* That gift became the pursuit, at all costs. The irony is that "serving God" by abandoning or neglecting the family, by failing to put bread on the table, or by overlooking key relationships so that the "dream" can be chased shakes down to simple irresponsibility and idolatry.

No talent is a substitute for the clear will of God. In fact, God may give us a gift in order to ask us to surrender it for a season.

Jesus modeled this better than anyone. He was gifted in *every* area. And yet he willingly set aside many of his abilities for a season in order to follow the will of God (see Phil. 2:5–8). One event in particular shows us how Jesus did it. To prepare for their last Passover together, Jesus told Peter and John to follow a man carrying water. This man would lead them to a house where they would request of the owner a guest room where Jesus could eat the Passover (see Mark 14:13–16; Luke 22:10–12). Notice *a servant with water* showed them the way to the upper room. But when Jesus and his disciples arrived at the upper room, no servant washed their feet. I think Jesus arranged it that way. He knew none of the disciples would volunteer for this menial task. Instead, they argued which of them was "regarded to be greatest" (Luke 22:24). Ironically, the greatest Person in the room took up the basin and towel and washed the feet of the whole group. How could he? Jesus had security in three areas—in who he was, in his relationship with the Father, and in where he was going (see John 13:3–5). Jesus could set aside his gifts and serve humbly because the source of his strength came from his inner assurance and security.

We may have a lot more to offer the world—perhaps even more to offer the kingdom of God—but is *more* the goal? Is maximizing our output our priority? When the daily and mundane responsibilities of life such as conversing with our spouse, or taking care of our health, or making time for our children seem to get in the way of our productivity, we need to stop and consider if productivity has become a way to justify personal fulfillment over personal faithfulness. Some of God's best work comes when he multiplies the fish and loaves of our faithfulness in doing a very little thing.

We may see ourselves as God's gift to humanity in our area of giftedness—maybe even the "greatest." But how willing are we to set aside that greatness for a season, as Jesus did, and wash feet? That's the real test of greatness. We can serve others from the same three areas of security that Jesus did—from who we are in Christ (see Rom. 8:1), from our relationship with the Father (see 1 John 2:23; Rev. 13:8), and in the confidence of where we are going (see Col. 1:5).

Yes, God wants to use us to change the world—but first he wants to change us. His primary work is *in* us, not *through* us. It always will be.

That's what the gaps are for. That's why we sit at God's stop-lights. That's why we do-si-do in the Round House. We think we're ready to move forward, but God sets us aside for a season. Why? To learn important lessons we would learn no other way. We see the setting-aside as a hindrance to progress. God sees it as an essential part of our development. He seems in no hurry during this season.

We may feel ready for a certain task, but God keeps the door closed. Instead he has us doing some boring and inane and ir-relevant assignment completely unrelated to our "purpose." But all along God is preparing *our character* for what he knows lies ahead—for a purpose we aren't yet ready to pursue. No one gives a rip about our giftedness if we're a jerk. Long-term influence comes as a byproduct of *character*.

What was true of Joseph remains true of us: "Until the time that his word came to pass, the word of the LORD tested him" (Ps. 105:19).

After my grandfather passed away years ago, we planted an oak tree in his memory in our front yard. The skinny stem stood more than six feet tall (just like Granddad did). A few hours later, I saw the tree leaning way over in the wind. I grabbed the trunk and gently bent the tree back. The whole base moved, because it had no root system yet. So I staked it down. Two years later when I bent the tree, the base didn't move. But you know what? The tree looked the same. Still as tall as Granddad. No higher. Its goal for its first two years was its roots, not its limbs and leaves.

All of us feel that daily tension to sideline our priorities. Our culture pushes its agenda even from the magazine racks: *Body Builder*, *Fashion*, *Vanity Fair*, and *Vogue*. We'll never see slick publications called *Popular Morality*, *Self-Control Digest*, *The*

Perseverance Report, or *Love Illustrated* (though that last one might sell a few). In the world we live in, it's all about the leaves. The roots are assumed.

This type of marketing yanks at our priorities. Too often, we'll follow the tug. To keep up appearances, we'll water our leaves and lengthen our limbs—and neglect our roots. We'll give priority to the visible and impressive and assume the unseen will care for itself. But our spiritual lives never take care of themselves. Nobody ever grows spiritually by accident. It is a daily decision.

The problem, of course, reveals itself when the wind blows. With only shallow roots below them, the leaves and limbs upend the whole tree—and it dies. Jesus spoke of this in his parable of the soils (see Matt. 13:20–21). Our externals often appear impressive: a decent income, comfortable cars, a good home, a fine-trimmed lawn, the latest clothes and techie gadgets. But what about the silent and unseen parts of our lives? What about the roots? Are they in place too? The taproot of life—our relationship with Jesus Christ—remains the silent, unseen, and yet essential source of what makes life really matter. Roots keep our tree standing tall when the wind rages.

"Let's go to the other side," Jesus told his disciples. His goal, of course, was not the other side of the Sea of Galilee as much as the journey to it. Halfway across the lake, a furious squall broke out and the apostles lost hope. And then, "Hush, be still!" the Master commanded (Mark 4:39). Oh, that all tests ended so quickly! Jesus calmed the storm in a moment, revealing his ability to do so—though he may choose not to do so in every storm. Remember, Jesus sent them *into* the storm—and thankfully, he also went with them.

Joseph saw the "other side" as God's promise to him revealed through his dreams. So he stood strong when the daily winds of temptation hurled a raging squall against him. When discouragement in the Round House threatened to uproot his confidence

106

in God's promise, Joseph didn't bend. His confidence remained rooted in God's revelation, and his relationship with God gave him a taproot from which he drew strength to keep going, to keep believing, and even to reach out to meet others' needs when his own needs seemed overwhelming.

These storms strengthened him, preparing him for a future God had for him.

But when?

6

The Opportunity of Obscurity

He who is faithful in a very little thing is faithful also in much.

Luke 16:10

I recently upgraded my smartphone and had a problem transferring my data to the new phone. So I called the company. As I talked to the tech during the data transfer, he really wanted to screen-share so he could see what was happening on my phone, but the connection wouldn't work. Because he couldn't see my screen, he continued to ask me every minute or so what the status read on my phone's progress bar. Finally, I said something like, "Look, continuing to ask me about it isn't going to speed up the process. Feel free to work on something else, and I'll let you know when it's done." Did he really think when it was completed I would say nothing?

Then it struck me. We do the same with God. In fact, God's people always have.

When Jesus's disciples asked him about the progress of God's kingdom, he reminded them of what we also need to remember. As much as we would like to know *when* progress will happen, God has determined we only need to know *what* we should be doing in the meantime (see Acts 1:7–8). It's almost as if God tells us what I told the tech: "Look, asking me about it isn't going to speed up the process. Feel free to work on something else, and I'll let you know when it's done." Do we really think when God is ready he will say nothing?

What good, then, did Joseph's ability to interpret dreams do for him? On the surface, not much—apparently it helped only the cupbearer, who enjoyed his promotion and promptly forgot the Hebrew guy. But actually it did much more than that.

I mentioned the officials' dreams served several purposes for Joseph. The first one came immediately with the opportunity to interpret the dreams, a test that served to show if Joseph had given up on his own dreams. *He hadn't.* The second purpose came three days later as Joseph's interpretations of their dreams came true. The point? *God had not forgotten Joseph's dreams either.* His correct interpretations of their dreams would have encouraged Joseph that his own dreams would still come true. God had not forgotten him! And there's one more purpose for the officials' dreams—a big one. (Coming soon.)

The many years of waiting had diminished nothing from God's promises to Joseph. *Nothing.* The same remains true for you and me. Joseph's life teaches us a wonderful principle: *God sees our faithfulness in obscurity as preparation for increasing influence.*

Think again about Jesus:

Who, although He existed in the form of God, did not regard equality with God a thing to be grasped, but emptied Himself, taking the form of a bond-servant. . . . For this reason also, God highly exalted Him, and bestowed on Him the name which is above every name. (Phil. 2:6–7, 9)

Jesus, God in the flesh, from the time he could hold a hammer until the time he was about thirty-three, labored as a carpenter. Talk about untapped potential! You mean the Son of God frittered away all those years driving nails and chiseling mortises when he could have healed people? Seems like a huge waste of time. On the contrary. Over the course of three and a half decades the Father prepared Jesus for a ministry of three and a half years. And because of his obedience—even to death on a cross—God exalted him to the highest place. Obedience in his obscurity led to increasing influence.

Joseph and Jesus weren't the only ones to experience this. Repeatedly in Scripture we see individuals who began with obscure faithfulness—people such as Ruth, David, Daniel, Esther, and Matthias—before God expanded their influence. In each case, God alone gave the promotion. He alone got the glory.

It's the same with us. When we beg God to rescue us from our insignificant lives, believing nothing important is happening to us, Joseph's story reminds us that just the opposite is true. We need to see our obscurity as a significant opportunity (see Matt. 25:21). Faithfulness in obscurity today puts us in a place of greater influence for God tomorrow. The biblical principle of sowing and reaping reveals we will usually experience a delay between our obedience to God and the harvest we reap: "Let us not lose heart in doing good, for in due time we will reap if we do not grow weary" (Gal. 6:9). Don't let the delay deceive you.

God knows our character will scale. "He who is faithful in a very little thing is faithful also in much," Jesus said, "and he who is unrighteous in a very little thing is unrighteous also in much" (Luke 16:10). Our daily walk with God offers no immediate maturity. It works to renew our minds and hearts over time, just as developing a good lawn takes years. Mowing. Weeding. Planting. Pulling. It takes many hard days of what seems like unproductive busywork to produce something beautiful. Maintenance and growth work together.

The sluggard in the book of Proverbs found his life suddenly ruined because he assumed "a little sleep, a little slumber" amounted to nothing (Prov. 24:33–34). But little things make up big things. Pennies make dollars. Bricks make walls. Days make years. Verses make Bibles. Little things matter, and when little things represent faithfulness to God, they remain crucial to our preparation for an expansion of our influence.

Unless we're careful, we can fall for the thinking that because what we do seems small, or behind-the-scenes, or insignificant, or unequal with our abilities or qualifications, what we do matters little. After all, if we foul up, no big deal. The world still turns. Nobody notices. Few seem to care.

Except God. People may forget us and forsake us, but "God is not unjust so as to forget your work" (Heb. 6:10).

"Lord, help me do great things as though they were little, since I do them with your powers," Pascal wrote, "and help me to do little things as though they were great, because I do them in your name."[1] What God wants for us in life requires more than our ability, giftedness, or education. It requires character. We go to school to acquire knowledge and skills. God takes us to his school to hammer out character.

His testing of our character brings situations that require integrity and evaluation of our intentions. These tests come in various shapes and on various levels.

⁓

The Lord was with Joseph, *and* Joseph remained forgotten for two years. Both are equally true. Now try saying it out loud with your name and your circumstance. The Lord is with (your name) *and* (your name) is in a difficult job . . . a challenging marriage . . . a financial hole. You get the idea. What you're saying is not a contradiction. God is with you in your struggle.

Oh, how we want God to be "with us"! But do we really? Do we really want Joseph's refining? Or all those maddening years circling in the Round House? Honestly, we often prefer a "safe" life that never gets us hurt. But that life also seldom recognizes God's hand. That's why he leads us, like it or not, along a path that includes struggle.

We always celebrate the faithfulness of God when life goes well. When asked in church or small groups to give testimony or praise, how often do we hear about God's faithfulness in the midst of an unresolved tragedy? We keep quiet about those—except to request prayer—and instead broadcast only resolutions as praises. But life doesn't always bring resolutions. If we believe God's Spirit indwells us and that he will never leave us nor forsake us, then we must factor God's faithfulness *during* those seasons when the bottom drops out of our lives.

When we face real-world pain, the promise of God's presence with us seems to offer very little. Like Gideon, we balk at the divine message that God is with us and answer as he did: "If the LORD is with us, why then has all this happened to us?" (Judg. 6:13). That's because we have a firm view of what God being with us looks like: no pain. But such a view treats the Scriptures as a buffet lunch where we pick and choose what we want to swallow about God. But when we do that, the plate we hold in our hands represents a god in our image—a freak unlike the God who tells us his ways are not like ours. Why would we want to worship a God we can control or understand? Where is the awe in that?

Joseph chose to recognize the truth: that God was with him *in* his circumstances. Joseph could have learned this principle from his father, who told Joseph's mother that success came from God being with him—in spite of circumstances that seemed against him (see Gen. 31:5). Joseph saw God with him in every one of his troubles. We know because he referred to God in each one.

God uses the seeming gaps of insignificance in our lives to develop our character. And the definition of character means more than morality. Character finds itself inseparably linked to our relationship with God. How do we deepen our relationship with God? We respond well to the trials he allows. If we don't learn the lessons the first lap around the Round House, we return and learn again. And again. Like a grade-school flunky, we will continue to wrestle against the fact that two plus two has only one answer. Until we get it, we'll never advance to fractions or algebra.

We cannot choose the ways in which we will struggle. God chooses those. But we can choose how we respond to those struggles. Struggle has meaning, but we don't have to understand the meaning. In fact, we will never fully grasp it. But not understanding the struggle has nothing to do with understanding that the struggle has a purpose—moreover, a good purpose. God's promises tell us so.

When we get frustrated that our lives seem to accomplish nothing or that our ministry bears little fruit, we need to review our motives for life and ministry. Rather than merely measure productivity and activity, we need to value the "little things," such as intentions, faithfulness, and faith. When we find ourselves dissatisfied with what God has us doing, it could reveal that we've confused our significance in serving God with our significance to God. Our relationship with God remains more important to him than our ministry for him. That is *huge*. We serve God from the overflow of our relationship with him, not as an aside to it.

If we have a shallow relationship with God, why would he enlarge the problem? Why grow the branches if the roots can't support them? The quality of our spiritual life is the quality of our whole life. Without exception.

About eleven years ago, I found myself in a season of obscurity, feeling rejected by friends who were closer to me than any others I had ever had. Everyone involved had good intentions, I believe. Nevertheless, when the music stopped playing, I was the one standing without a chair at the ministry where I had served for fourteen years. After hearing about my sudden and surprising transition, a neighbor of ours asked Cathy and me if we had any verses we were claiming during this season. "Yeah," I answered, "Genesis 37 through 50."

Joseph has always been my favorite Bible character (other than Jesus), but he became an especially good friend during that winter season. And although I hope never to go through those feelings of aloneness again, I also treasure what God taught me about his faithfulness during those many months. Namely, our obscurity offers us a tremendous opportunity—a season we dare not miss.

Joseph saw what seemed to contradict God's promise as an opportunity to demonstrate faith—not a reason to doubt or abandon it.

If God has you in a place where your gifts are not fully utilized, or if you feel set aside in God's grand plan, or if those around you have marginalized you, trivialized you, or flat-out rejected you, I understand how tough that is.

But you're not stuck. God isn't done with you. If he were, you'd be dead.

You may experience some days in life when you really, really don't think you can hold out. The weight of disappointment feels far heavier and more real than the promise of God that lies beyond it. Enduring a difficult situation seems impossible until you realize you only have to make it through the day. Then tomorrow, through that day. (Of course, this doesn't apply in an abusive situation.) Do this one day at a time, and you'll wake up one day with the reality that you've endured a difficult situation for five, ten, even fifty years. Some people call that ridiculous. Crazy. A waste of life.

God calls it perseverance.

We glorify God by standing up under a heavy load. "If when you do what is right and suffer for it you patiently endure it," Peter writes, "this finds favor with God" (1 Pet. 2:20). The victorious Christian life is not a life without struggle. Victory presupposes a battle. The victory in the Christian life comes as a victory of choice and attitude in the midst of a life that suffers. The quality of life rests in our attitude, not in our circumstances. To *realize* something is to consider it to be *real*. And when you realize endurance finds favor with God, it can bring peace and joy to any troubled situation.

Sometimes the path to greater influence includes what seem like setbacks. But they aren't. God simply uses these tensions to propel us forward. Like an arrow pulled back against the bow. Occasionally God sidelines us to remind us our participation is a privilege and we can glorify him just as much by our waiting on him as by our serving him in some other way that feels more fulfilling to us.

God takes delight in using us, but he doesn't need us. He got along just fine in eternity past as Father, Son, and Spirit. His plan worked well long before we stepped on the scene, and it won't skip a beat after we're gone.

Our limitations only frustrate us when we forget that in weakness we glorify God. For example, a husband or wife will surrender massive amounts of time to marriage and parenting, understanding that God is in no way limited by this limitation. Other desires are limited, for sure, but that may be precisely why God wanted us to get married and have kids. How else would we face our selfishness unless we had to? Consider the untimely deaths of Blaise Pascal, David Brainerd, Jonathan Edwards, Dietrich Bonhoeffer, and Keith Green—to name but a few. They all died in their prime, and yet, their short lives have offered the kingdom of God much more than many whole lives lived unsurrendered. Just as God can take the life of someone with so much potential—and use their brief life span for his glory—so he can use the limited time offered by a husband or wife who understands marriage and family as a primary way to glorify God (see 1 Cor. 7:32–35). To resist or resent the time God's priorities require amounts to resisting God.

God experiences no limitation by our limitations. He needs no sleep, has to earn no living, nor has any shortage of time or space. We, on the other hand, have all of these confines—including our battle with our sinful nature. Even on our best days, we offer God only scraps to work with—only fish and loaves that he somehow multiplies to make adequate.

Waiting on God reminds us of those facts. Waiting keeps us humble. Waiting shows us over the passing of time that it's all about God and none of it is about us—except to the degree that we glorify him. Remember, the goal is God's glory, not our productivity or personal fulfillment. In our waiting, God weans us from the pride of having to control everything or understand matters "too difficult for" us (Ps. 131:1). God chooses how we glorify him. He alone selects which of his servants will produce what levels of output—and yet, he also rewards faithfulness on any level with *equal* commendation (see Matt. 25:14–23).

God works through our waiting to strengthen our character through weakness, to develop our peace of mind by trusting him in chaos, and to teach us that we can glorify him just as much by waiting on him as we can by serving him. When we choose to find our fulfillment in his glory, then we can wait on him to open the doors of greater influence in his time. That's really his business entirely. Ours is to live faithfully wherever he puts us now.

When Jesus's brothers pressured him to quit wasting time in obscurity and to head to Jerusalem to become famous, his answer to them could also apply to us: "My time is not yet here, but your time is always opportune" (John 7:6). We often want greater influence immediately, but God wants it appropriately. For us, the best solution often seems the quickest one. But with God, the best time comes "at the proper time" (1 Pet. 5:6).

God's timing knows its own reasons. Perhaps the delay occurs to test how seriously we will pray. Or maybe, in spite of all we've learned, God still has more to teach us. Or maybe the answer to God's delay has little to do with us at all—because it depends on someone else responding to God.

Whatever the reasons, I'm convinced that in most cases God delays because he wants to give us more than we're asking for. He loves us enough to wait to give us his best rather than to satisfy our impatience with a quick, cheap substitute. That's why we mustn't equate his delay with a deaf ear.

Sometimes what seems like God's apathy is really his mercy. It was that way with Joseph.

The cupbearer forgot Joseph. Imagine what would have happened if the cupbearer *had* remembered Joseph. Likely, Pharaoh would have disregarded the issue altogether. But best-case scenario, Pharaoh would have released Joseph and allowed him to return home to Hebron. What's wrong with that? The happy story of a son restored to his father would have ended a few years later as they all died of starvation in the upcoming famine. God knew about the famine. Nobody else did. God allowed the cupbearer to forget Joseph and allowed Joseph to wait—disappointed, disillusioned, and confused—so that he could receive an answer far better than he imagined.

After the cupbearer forgot Joseph, he languished two more years in the Round House. Two *full years*. That's 104 weeks. That's 730 days. That's 17,520 hours. I won't even count the minutes. Joseph had hoped the cupbearer was God's answer to prayer. And he was. It just took a lot longer than Joseph expected. It took waiting on God.

Then one day it all changed.

Finally, the Round House had a corner to turn.

"Now it happened at the end of two full years that Pharaoh had a dream" (Gen. 41:1).

The king of Egypt joined the ranks of those God spoke to in dreams. But the Lord cloaked the meaning of the dreams behind strange metaphors: seven gaunt cows swallowing up seven fat cows, and seven thin ears of grain consuming seven plump ears. Offbeat dreams for sure. But they were more than dog dreams. Something about them nagged the king.

When he revealed his dreams to his Egyptian magicians, they just shrugged their shoulders. All of his wise men and their gods had nothing to say. He felt desperate to understand his visions, but he had no one to help him.

Suddenly, a light went on in the cupbearer's brain.

He remembered Joseph.

The cupbearer described to Pharaoh how a young Hebrew had correctly interpreted his and the baker's dreams when they were in prison together, two years earlier. Pharaoh stared with amazement. Someone could interpret his dreams?

Imagine how quickly events transpired in the next few minutes.

Joseph awoke that morning as he always had and clanked across the room to begin the humdrum tasks he had done thousands of times. Then he heard loud voices in the distance. He stood still to listen to the commotion. The voices got louder and louder until they stood just outside the prison door. Then came the clinking of keys, the snap of the lock, the creak of the door as it opened and banged against the prison wall.

Several officials with torches squinted inside and scanned the scrubby prisoners in the Round House. The cupbearer broke the silence. "That's him!"

He was pointing at Joseph.

Hands trembled with haste as they located the tool that unlocked Joseph's iron collar and unfastened his leg irons. As the chains slid into a pile on the floor, they pulled Joseph out the door, his feet barely touching the ground as they carried him along, running.

For the first time in many years, Joseph's chains were silent.

A quick shave, a change of clothes, and a crash course on protocol had Joseph standing before the most powerful man in the world. Pharaoh inspected the Hebrew through deep-sunken eyes, bloodshot from a tough night's sleep. Joseph's heart pounded as he stood, waiting. Finally, Pharaoh spoke.

"I have had a dream, but no one can interpret it; and I have heard it said about you, that when you hear a dream you can interpret it" (v. 15).

"I cannot do it," Joseph replied. Hearing this, the cupbearer must have gasped and stiffened, anticipating another extended vacation in the Round House. But then Joseph added, "But God will give Pharaoh the answer he desires" (v. 16 NIV).

Joseph's first words out of prison pointed to God.

Joseph had the same response two years earlier when speaking to the cupbearer and the baker about their dreams (see 40:8). As we've seen, the officials' dreams served several purposes for Joseph. Initially, they tested him to see if he had given up on his own dreams. He hadn't forsaken them. Three days later, Joseph's correct interpretations would have encouraged him that God had not forsaken him. And finally, these accurate interpretations served as the catalyst for placing Joseph before Pharaoh at this moment.

We never know who will prove significant in our lives. We have *no* clue. Those we presumed would make all the difference often turn out to be duds. Instead, God frequently uses unimportant or unexpected people as the means of significant transitions. And so it happened with Joseph. God had honored Joseph's faithfulness in the little things. Now he would honor Joseph's faithfulness with expanded influence.

"God will give Pharaoh the answer he desires." As Pharaoh shared his two dreams with Joseph, God revealed their meanings to Joseph, who then reiterated them to Pharaoh. The two dreams saw life and death, just as the two dreams of the cupbearer and the baker did. Joseph had two dreams too—one of sheaves bowing down. It's interesting how these three sets of dreams have similar elements.

Joseph relayed the meaning of Pharaoh's dreams. The seven lean cows and seven thin ears of grain represented a seven-year famine that would swallow up seven previous years of abundance. Then Joseph went beyond what Pharaoh asked of him and offered a wise course of action to prepare for the effects of the famine. He suggested Pharaoh appoint a wise man to oversee and stockpile the coming abundance of grain in order to prepare for the famine that would follow.

Even if we had never read the story before, we shouldn't be surprised at who Pharaoh chose to be that man. Back in Canaan, Jacob had put Joseph in charge as a seventeen-year-old boy. Then Potiphar put Joseph in command of his house. Next, the jailer put him in charge of the prisoners in the Round House. And now, of course, Pharaoh assigned Joseph the position of prime minister over the entire land of Egypt.

> Pharaoh said to Joseph, "Though I am Pharaoh, yet without your permission no one shall raise his hand or foot in all the land of Egypt." Then Pharaoh named Joseph Zaphenath-paneah; and he gave him Asenath, the daughter of Potiphera priest of On, as his wife. . . . Now Joseph was thirty years old when he stood before Pharaoh, king of Egypt. And Joseph went out from the presence of Pharaoh and went through all the land of Egypt. (Gen. 41:44–46)

As Joseph rode throughout Egypt in Pharaoh's chariot, all the people knelt before him in homage. I wonder what went through

Potiphar's and his wife's minds as they bowed before Joseph. Interestingly, the last three promotions in Joseph's life transpired because an unbeliever noticed the hand of God upon Joseph.

The probable meaning of the Egyptian name Pharaoh gave Joseph, *Zaphenath-paneah*, matches Joseph's own consistent testimony about his Lord: "God speaks and lives."

Have you ever noticed how much can happen in a day? Sometimes it seems more happens in a day than in a month. That's because most major transitions in life turn a corner without slowing down. Joseph's story proves that.

Mapping Joseph's life plots a series of hard U-turns. One hour Joseph rides in the sun wearing his multicolored coat, and the next hour he squats in a dark cistern half-naked. One week he strolls in his father's tents, and the next he lies strapped to a camel on a long trip to Egypt. One day he oversees the household of an Egyptian official, and the next he finds himself imprisoned in the same house. One day he's a dirty prisoner, and the next he's an unsoiled prime minister. Instead of an iron collar, Joseph now sports a gold necklace. Instead of wearing threadbare prison rags, he now stands clothed in fine linen. Instead of itchy inches of untrimmed beard, Joseph now rubs his rough hands over the smooth skin of a clean-shaven face. Instead of manacles on his legs, he now wears the signet ring of Pharaoh on his hand. From riches to rags and now back to riches. How things had changed! Again, all in one day.

Joseph came to Egypt as a seventeen-year-old boy, and now, the Bible tells us, he stood before Pharaoh as a thirty-year-old man (see Gen. 37:2; 41:46). Like me, you've probably already done the math—and we're supposed to. The Bible gives us these reference points as more than incidental matters of curiosity. By giving us his ages, Scripture reminds us that—in spite of Joseph's amazing turning points—most of life is gaps.

Most of life is waiting on God.

In the long, thirteen-year gap that included betrayals, temptations, shackles, injustices, struggles, questions, and many months of awful silence, God had refined and prepared Joseph. Although it could appear Joseph had wasted his time as a slave and as a prisoner, in truth, God had wasted no event to prepare his man for this moment. During the past thirteen years, Joseph had become fluent in the Egyptian dialect. Through two different positions of responsibility, he had learned how to harvest abundant crops, to manage a large staff, to lead, to organize, to do a lot with a little, to deal with difficult people—and he had done it all well, with God's blessing.

Others intended evil for Joseph, but Joseph learned to see the bigger picture. God was at work. He intended it all for good.

What's more, Joseph was learning to wait on God.

How do we know? Before this moment, the last words we heard from Joseph's lips requested the cupbearer to appeal Joseph's case to Pharaoh. And yet, when Joseph stood before Pharaoh, the young Hebrew made no personal request. Not one. He said nothing of his kidnapping or his false imprisonment as he had earlier to the cupbearer. Furthermore, the moment Joseph had power in Egypt, he could have requested from Pharaoh a quick trip to Hebron to reunite with his father and to inform him of his wellbeing. But amazingly, Joseph did none of that. Not even a courier sent. That amazes me.

Somehow in the past two years of waiting, Joseph had learned that God would bring about his will in his time—and in his way. He needed no help. Not even from those in powerful government positions.

And believe it or not, God still had more refining to do in Joseph's life. Although Genesis slips a veil over what the purifying involved, Psalm 105 reveals the endpoint that God's specific refining would reach: "Until the time that his word came to pass, the word of the LORD tested him" (v. 19). In other words, just because Joseph has gone from rags to riches, we shouldn't think God has fulfilled his dreams. Not yet. Joseph's dreams—"his word"—said nothing about ruling over Egypt but rather of ruling over his family.

As it turned out, Joseph still had more waiting to do.

In reality, Joseph's success now offered him another refining test. Now that Joseph has "arrived," would he give up on his dreams? After all, life couldn't get much better than this.

Let's pause and consider that Moses originally wrote Genesis (as well as Exodus, Leviticus, Numbers, and Deuteronomy) for readers who lived hundreds of years after Joseph. As the redeemed Hebrew nation anticipated reentering Canaan, the Lord issued them an important warning:

> When the LORD your God brings you into . . . great and splendid cities which you did not build, and houses full of all good things which you did not fill, and hewn cisterns which you did not dig, vineyards and olive trees which you did not plant, and you eat and are satisfied, then watch yourself, that you do not forget the LORD who brought you from the land of Egypt, out of the house of slavery. (Deut. 6:10–12)

Notice God's emphasis by the repeated phrase "which you did not." The blessings his people would receive would come from God's hand—not from their own wits or wisdom. Moses warned his nation of prosperity's greatest temptation: to forget God, who redeemed them from slavery.

Of course, Joseph had never read Deuteronomy. But he fit the bill, didn't he? He was a former Egyptian slave living in abundance in a pagan land. Joseph stood as the leader of the world's leading superpower. Plus, he was young, gifted, intelligent, good-looking, and extremely wealthy. How do most young men in our culture act who come into this kind of windfall? Think of pro athletes or even superstars who began on YouTube. Can you name many who still walk with God?

You and I are rich too, by the way—and I mean more than spiritually. Many of us have a garbage disposal that eats better than much of the world's population. Prosperity and blessings are ours in abundance—and tempt us to neglect God. Of course, we don't *want* to overlook him, but if we don't "watch ourselves," we will.

Our quiet time with God, for example, remains an act of faith. Bible reading brings few quick fixes, and prayer seldom reveals shafts of light. Instead, growth takes time—like roots making their way deep into the earth. How tempting every day to skirt our time with God and instead to rush toward the urgent tasks on our endless lists! But little things make up big things, remember?

Unless we watch ourselves, we will allow our busy lives to drift away from our devotion to Jesus Christ. We will adore our families, our homes, our jobs, our ministries, our vacations, our salvation—all of God's blessings to us. But before we know it, we can replace devotion to the Lord with devotion to his blessings. And in sad, twisted irony, those blessings become our focus instead of the God who gave them.

Our walk with God is not an appointment we keep each day— and then move on—like climbing the rungs of a ladder. Instead, our time with him forms the foundation that supports *all* we do. We stand on it. We build on it. We don't climb past it.

Would Joseph forget God? During the seven years of abundance, Joseph gathered so much grain in cities and storehouses that he stopped measuring it. We hear nothing from Joseph during these seven long years of prosperity until just before they end.

Then we see it.

Pharaoh had given Joseph a pagan wife, Asenath, the daughter of a pagan priest. How interesting that the first person Joseph would become close to represented the complete antithesis of everything he believed. Though we can put no stock in the apocryphal novel written many centuries later, *Joseph and Asenath*, the story relates how Joseph's wife came to faith in the true God. Though the novel itself is pure fiction, it likely got this point right. Because Asenath had no effect on Joseph's faith, he likely affected hers.

Just before the years of famine, Joseph and Asenath had two sons. After all these years of prosperity, and after speaking Egyptian for twenty years, Joseph chose to give his sons Hebrew names, both of which gave glory to God. In naming his firstborn Manasseh, Joseph gave God credit as the One who had made him "forget all my trouble and all my father's household" (Gen. 41:51). Joseph named his second son Ephraim, meaning "fruitfulness," for Joseph said, "God has made me fruitful in the land of my affliction" (v. 52).

Joseph had not forgotten God, even in success.

Most of us can relate easier to Joseph in prison than to Joseph in the palace. Our blessings notwithstanding, most of us will never experience the superstar status and magnificent wealth Joseph had. We live somewhere in between the prison and the palace, a pendulum that swings on the axis of our minds.

Circumstances always change our minds about God. They either tempt us to doubt what he has promised or draw us closer to him in faith. But we never stay the same. As cruel as it may seem at first, God's plan for us includes the struggles we face today. That doesn't mean God approves the evil done to us any more than the Lord sanctioned the abuse from Joseph's dysfunctional family. It does mean, however, that God promises to use every experience he allows in our lives for our good—if we are Christians (see Gen. 50:20; Rom. 8:28).

It's important we remember that our goal in our struggles lies outside of trying to understand God's plan. We'll never do it.

Furthermore, he never asks that of us. Instead, he wants to see our trust in him through simple daily obedience in little things. Little things often begin in little places.

When we see ourselves in a place of obscurity, our dependence on God remains obvious. We pray for the Lord to keep us faithful and for the Spirit of God to lead us forward as it pleases him to do so. We hold our place in the world with open hands, trusting God to do with us as he chooses. But honestly, it's easy to hold with open hands something we don't want anyway—or something we see as insignificant. It's easy to let go of one rung to grab a higher one as we make our way upward.

But once we reach our goal, once God graciously has enlarged our influence to a broader level, once he has given us the platform we feel ready to assume, it becomes tough to release *that* rung—and to give it back to God should he require it. This place of blessing can be many things: a spouse, a child, a position, a ministry, a best friend, anything or anyone we love so much we hesitate to open our hands to God.

If we don't watch ourselves—as God warned the Hebrews—in our very vulnerable place of attainment and blessing, we can forget the God who blessed us. In extreme examples, we can even morph into control freaks. After all, so much success requires so much maintenance—and we have to police how it all happens lest we jeopardize the very success that brought us here. In the next chapter, we'll see this occurring in Jacob's life—*again*. It had already occurred with Jacob's inordinate love for Joseph, and it would happen once more with Jacob's new idol—his son Benjamin. It would come as a hard lesson. It comes the same to us.

Along with our fear of surrendering what God gave us comes a predictable, slumbering apathy toward the spiritual life. This inclination usually piggybacks on the sheer busyness of our success. We have to keep the cogs greased. We simply no longer have time for the little things. Like people. Or personal holiness. Or God.

But we see none of this in Joseph. Notice he gave Hebrew names to his sons at the height of his prosperity, not in the years of famine. Joseph remained the same person in the palace as he was in the prison. He chose to remain faithful wherever God had placed him, knowing the Lord would open the doors of his promises in his time. Success for Joseph occurred long before he ruled Egypt.

Joseph grew to understand that God sees *faithfulness*—on any level—as success.

That begs a question: Exactly for whose applause do we live and serve? If for God alone, then we can find contentment in our seemingly obscure place. But if for people (including ourselves), then stadiums full of fans chanting our name will never be enough. If we're honest, we often serve God more for ourselves than for him. Like James and John, we want Jesus to give us the best seats in the house—the most significant places of service in God's kingdom (see Mark 10:37). The most—*whatever*. But Scripture shows us that Christ will evaluate our lives based on the quality, not the quantity, of our work and our motives (see 1 Cor. 3:13; 4:5). If God's glory really is the goal, then maybe we need to do less but do it better, rather than keep shoveling more activity onto the high pile of mediocrity.

As we wait on God, we need to adopt the philosophy of work and ministry that Joseph modeled. We need to choose to stay faithful in the position of life God has placed us now—whether it seems big or little.

What about you?

Let's say you have followed God's leading faithfully. Perhaps you've earned an advanced degree but no position opens up. Instead, you find yourself in a no-name company doing a menial job and contributing nothing of significant value. Or let's suppose you have raised your children and now the empty nest has given you empty days of nothingness in which you'd love to serve God if only he would show you where. Or you retired years ago and you feel set aside by the world and by the Lord. You're ready for a change. You've asked God to open a new door in your life, and he has taken years to prepare you for it. You're ready. You're willing.

But nothing happens.

It's a tough place to be. Your situation is different, of course, but your reaction should remain the same. In those moments when you ask yourself, *Why isn't God using me?* you really mean to ask, *Why isn't God using me like I want to be used?* It seems like you have so much potential just sitting on the sidelines.

And you do. Your opportunity is huge. It's right in front of you.

Sometimes the dreams and goals you have for life are good goals, even godly goals—but just not God's goals. Your expectations of life are just that—*yours*. God has his own set of plans, and he reveals them only step by step.

God may initially lead you in one direction simply to take you in another. He may give you a vision as a single, or for a family, or for a ministry only so that he can sanctify you by his grace in experiencing a slammed door. Slammed doors do more than bend your nose; they keep your heart pliable, sensitive, and available to God's leading. Not only does he keep secret the difficult valleys you'll experience (and many of the mountaintops) but also the tremendous lessons you'll glean no other way. Lessons you didn't know you needed to learn. Lessons you'll thank him for one day.

You may fail to recognize God using you significantly because you define God "using you" in terms of what you consider significant: *results*. But God often defines results in terms of character. Words like *productivity* and *efficiency* remain conspicuously absent from the fruit of the Spirit (see Gal. 5:22–23). These results of God working in your life all reflect character—his character. Character alone produces godly results.

Sometimes you may find it necessary to set your gift on the shelf for a while and focus on other parts of God's will for your life. These seasons force a question: *What has my heart above all else, my gifts or the Giver?* God may ask you to set something aside for a season in order to develop another area (like character) or another gift altogether. In fact, the setting-aside season can foster such significant growth that it may make the gift even more effective when God finally opens the door for its use.

If your heart feels a tug toward the big things everyone sees, remember Joseph. The Lord takes more interest in the little things only he sees. Why? Little things reveal the heart—the platform of true success.

In whatever obscure place you find yourself today, you can be sure of this: God is with you, just as he was with Joseph, and God is working to develop your character in the little things.

We call it obscurity. God calls it opportunity. The little things remain available to you right now—right where you live today.

Sometimes the blessing of obscurity comes with a simple change of perspective. You know, you already have a *huge* fan base.

You have an audience of One—*God.*

He is applauding.

7

THE SURPRISING PLACE
WHERE WAITING BEGINS

*Their hearts sank, and they turned trembling to one another,
saying, "What is this that God has done to us?"*

Genesis 42:28

Our daily walk with God includes a whole lot of waiting on him. It always will. A life of faith, hope, and love requires a life of waiting. But it never began there. It began with God waiting on us.

As Creator, God made the first move. We, as creatures, responded—by disobeying. He sought us out with a way of redemption. We, as sinners, responded—by believing. We love because he first loved us. We did not choose him; he chose us. He came to seek and save the lost. We come to him only because he drew us in the first place (see Gen. 1:27–28; 3:9; Luke 19:10; John 6:44; 15:16; 1 John 4:19).

See the pattern? In every interaction with God, he took the lead—and then he waited for us to respond.

This really hasn't changed, even for us as believers. The life we live as Christians is a life that responds and corresponds to the life of Christ within us, to the promptings of the Holy Spirit, and to the commands God initiated in Scripture. Even when we do seek God, it's by his command (see Ps. 27:8).

The Lord takes the initiative in our lives and he waits for us to respond. In the process of this divine exchange, we grow. And part of God's initiative in these events gets really uncomfortable.

When God chooses to test our faith, the test shows up unexpectedly. Like a pop quiz. We never see it coming. If we knew we faced a big test next week, we'd prepare ahead of time. We'd brace ourselves for the unexpected and get really spiritual—*fast*.

But that's not a real test.

A real test blindsides us. When God drops a quiz in our laps, it's like catching a live grenade. We have only an instant to choose our response. Sometimes an embarrassing kneejerk reaction kicks in before we have time to think about it. I remember one such test.

Years ago, one of my daughters went with me to buy dog food. As we walked into the pet store, the employee behind the counter saw us, and immediately his face lit up. "Are you Wayne Stiles?" he asked.

Surprised, I said, "Yes."

Okay, pause this scene. In that moment, my brain's kneejerk reaction (emphasis on *jerk*) immediately chased the possible reasons this complete stranger knew my name. *Maybe he read something I wrote, or perhaps he heard me speak, or maybe he . . .* and the list went on—but I won't. All this shot through my mind in an instant. (Don't you just hate it when God drags his yard rake across the soil of your heart and unearths all kinds of junk just below the surface? Everything seems smooth, and suddenly, up pops the equivalent of a beer can, exposing your fault.) Now, un-pause the scene.

The guy behind the counter revealed how he knew my name. "Your wife just called. You're supposed to call home."

Up popped a beer can in my heart.

As it turned out, he recognized me because Cathy told him I would have my five-year-old daughter with me. It had *nothing* to do with anything I said, wrote, or did. You know what galled me most about this event? I innocently walked into a store to buy dog food, and God handed me a pop quiz that exposed the pride hidden beneath the surface of my heart.

Let's be honest. When someone says to us, "Hey, a friend of mine said something nice about you today," how do we respond? If we can contain our spontaneous elation, we may casually answer like it's no big deal. But inside? We're dying to know what that someone said about us.

Honestly, most of the tests God issues us come as sucker punches to our pride followed by a spinning Bruce Lee–style kick to our hypocrisy. We never see them coming because they hit our blind spots. Suddenly we're humbled by what the tests reveal: we are not the person we think we are. But neither are we the person God will help us become.

The Lord also hands us other tests. Bigger ones. These examine the mettle of our theology and often even seem to contradict it. They find more than the beer cans that surprise us in kneejerk moments of pride. They unearth the *trash can* full of empties we ourselves have buried deep below the surface. These exacting exams go beyond our blind spots to places we turn a blind eye to. Oh, we see them all right. We just pretend we don't.

But we know right where we buried them. So does God.

The seven years of plenty came to an end, and the seven years of famine began—just as Joseph predicted. Once again, Joseph took reassurance from God that he could interpret dreams. Moreover, Joseph knew God would bring about the fulfillment of his own dreams in time. He only had to wait on God.

Fast-forward two years.

The severe famine had ravaged the land, and the Egyptians looked to Pharaoh for help. The king pointed them to Joseph, who unlocked the storehouses and sold grain both to the Egyptians and to all who came to Egypt from nearby lands.

These years of famine had taken their toll in Canaan as well. Jacob heard from travelers that Egypt had grain for sale. He looked at his sons and asked, "Why do you just keep looking at each other?" (Gen. 42:1 NIV). Classic line. In other words, "Why don't you guys do something about our situation?" No answer.

Jacob told his sons to go buy grain in Egypt. But he sent only ten of them. He refused to send Joseph's brother Benjamin. Why? "Jacob did not send Benjamin, Joseph's brother, with the others, because he was afraid that harm might come to him" (v. 4 NIV).

Ah, déjà vu. In those words we catch a glimpse of what life has been like in Hebron for the past twenty-two years. Jacob found a new favorite son to replace Joseph. Jacob had lost one darling and he wasn't about to lose another. This youngest son remained the only child from his favorite wife, Rachel. Benjamin would not go to Egypt. It would be like Rachel dying all over again. No way.

The insinuation in Jacob's words rang loud and clear to the older brothers: "Harm can befall one of you guys—and that's okay. You're expendable. But Benjamin is special. He stays here."

The ten brothers who had fumed with jealousy over Joseph had solved nothing by selling him into slavery. Daddy had just picked a new Joseph. Jacob's loss only made him cling more tightly to Rachel's remaining son. With their father doting over Benjamin, the other ten sons had to stomach a day-by-day reminder of their sin—for the past twenty-two years.

No wonder Judah had left.

Yet, as we saw with Judah earlier, God refused to allow him to forget Joseph. And at some point, many years later, Judah returned to Hebron. Maybe he realized he couldn't escape the elephant in the room by running away. Perhaps he returned after his slipup with Tamar. Or possibly the famine forced him home. Who knows? God can use any means.

And although Genesis highlights only Judah's experiences during these ensuing years, the other brothers also would have their own stories—unrecorded gaps in the narrative, but they're there nonetheless. All of the sons had hoped the beer cans they buried would stay hidden, but God has a big rake. Just as with Judah, all of their consciences remained unsettled because the Lord had allowed no resolution.

Not yet.

Jacob had dispatched Joseph to travel alone on multiple occasions, but now the old man refused to let Benjamin travel even in the safety of ten other men. Imagine what life was like for Benjamin. The protective father refused to allow his son to leave his side. What a way to grow up.

So, the same ten brothers who sold Joseph into slavery in Egypt headed to Egypt themselves to buy grain. Finally, for the first time since the brothers' cruel deed to Joseph, the elephant in the room vacated Hebron—and it traveled with the ten to Egypt.

Joseph had sold grain to thousands of people by this time, from all neighboring lands. Yet when his brothers appeared and bowed in homage before him, he immediately recognized them even after twenty-two years. Furthermore, he "remembered the dreams which he had about them" (v. 9). They, of course, had no clue he was Joseph; they only saw Egypt's powerful prime minister.

Joseph used the disguise and began the dialogue.

The last time Joseph had spoken to his brothers, their words had been harsh, cold, and callous. Employing an interpreter, Joseph spoke to his brothers with a deliberate, severe tone and questioned them about where they came from. Then he accused them of spying on Egypt! Understand, Joseph's words weren't vindictive. He wasn't using his position for payback. Far from it. God's refining of Joseph's character had taught him to wait on God, and the Lord's testing of Joseph—"until the time that his word came to pass" (Ps. 105:19)—had led to this moment. Joseph's purpose had to do with a much bigger plan. And he knew it.

The sight of his brothers prompted Joseph to remember his dreams, the first of which came true the moment he laid eyes on them. They bowed before him. *Dream one: check.*

But Joseph had two dreams, the second of which required Benjamin and his father as well.

When Joseph accused them of coming as spies, the allegation forced them to explain their place of origin. "Your servants are twelve brothers in all," they answered, "the sons of one man in the land of Canaan; and behold, the youngest is with our father today, and one is no longer alive" (Gen. 42:13). Their words gave Joseph the first opportunity in years to hear his native dialect. He used an interpreter, and yet he understood better than the translator—every nuance of facial expression, each emphasis of syllable, every underlying tone from personalities he knew as well as his own.

"One is no more," they said (NIV). *Ouch.* I wonder how that phrase landed on Joseph. They thought by now Joseph was certainly dead, yet there he stood before them, a thirty-nine-year-old man!

Joseph could put two and two together. He knew the jealousy that had sent him to Egypt. He also understood why Benjamin hadn't come. But one thing he didn't know: Had his brothers changed? Or did they still have jealous, malicious hearts?

There was only one way to find out.

136

"By this you will be tested," Joseph demanded. "Send one of you that he may get your brother, while you remain confined" (vv. 15–16). By calling the experience a "test," Joseph gave them more than a mere opportunity to prove they weren't spies. He already knew that. But they had claimed themselves "honest men" (v. 11). Really? Simeon and Levi had murdered the Shechemites in revenge; Reuben had tried to grab his preeminence early through incest; Judah had refused his obligation to give his son away in marriage and then slept with a harlot (or so he thought); and the whole lot of them had sold a brother into slavery out of jealousy and then lied about it. Are these honest men?

But maybe they had changed. If not, perhaps they would be willing to. Maybe God had used the past twenty-two years in their lives just as he had in Joseph's.

Joseph put them in prison for three days—perhaps even in the Round House—all together in the same place. This began the "test"—the Lord's pop quiz for these men. Their words to Joseph, "one is no more," would have ignited the kindling in their consciences over what they had done. These ten brothers had three days and nights in prison to stare at the walls, at one another, and at their ubiquitous pet elephant. More than a beer can or two popped up as God dragged his rake across their hearts. They were imprisoned in the confines of their guilt, and God began to exhume the dead brother they had tried to keep buried for twenty-two years.

These three days also gave Joseph some time to think, to pray, and to improve his plan. He then brought them out of prison and explained the next steps. Instead of having only one brother return for Benjamin, Joseph chose only one to stay imprisoned. That allowed more men to carry more grain back to the family. But one part of the plan Joseph kept the same.

He required they bring Benjamin to Egypt.

The new favorite son would have to leave the father. Joseph knew he had struck a nerve with his demand as he overheard them talking to each other.

"Truly we are guilty concerning our brother, because we saw the distress of his soul when he pleaded with us, yet we would not listen," they said, "therefore this distress has come upon us" (v. 21). Then Reuben, the one who had tried to restore Joseph to his father, shot back, "Did I not tell you, 'Do not sin against the boy'; and you would not listen? Now comes the reckoning for his blood" (v. 22).

Three days of imprisonment in their guilty consciences had done its work. These men, who twenty-two years ago had brutally betrayed Joseph, now began to admit what they did was wrong. They had seen Joseph's distress, they had heard Reuben's warning, but they had refused to listen. They understood they were now reaping the consequences.

They were beginning to see God's initiative in their lives.

Of course, Joseph understood every word, and his emotions welled up so much he had to turn away. He had named his firstborn son Manasseh because the Lord had helped him forget the pain of his family, and yet these few words opened a floodgate of feelings. God can bring healing, but memories can still bring tears.

With his harsh face back in place, Joseph reappeared and had Simeon tied in front of them all and returned him to the prison. Joseph also secretly had their money returned in their grain sacks, which one of them discovered on the way back to Hebron. This marked the second time they would come home with money that wasn't theirs—the first time occurred after selling their brother as a slave.

They interpreted the event correctly and spoke to one another with trembling throats: "What is this that God has done to us?" (v. 28).

Answer: God was taking the initiative. Now he was waiting on them to respond.

A few weeks before my forty-fifth birthday, my body gave me a little gift. I awoke suddenly one night with a smarting pain in my lower back. No matter how much I fidgeted and squirmed, the hurt only intensified.

The best way I can describe the pain compares to having a doctor insert a three-inch hypodermic needle to the left of the spine, just below where the kidney sits. Occasionally, just for fun, the doc then twists the needle in a slow, clockwise motion. The pain literally nauseated me. Never before had I experienced such an inescapable ache. More frightening than the pain was the fact that I had no idea why it was happening.

As I described the symptoms to a doctor friend of mine the following day, he said it sounded like a kidney stone. *It's probably just a kidney infection*, I thought, *not a kidney stone*. As a boy, I had watched my father struggle to pass a kidney stone, and it wasn't pretty. From my perspective as a kid, I thought his kidney stone just came from being old. And since I was not old when my pain struck, I felt safe. Perfectly logical.

A couple of days later, I sat in the urologist's office. He strolled in, shook my hand, and announced in a ho-hum manner, "You have a kidney stone." Holding up my X-ray, he pointed to a small, delta-shaped blip between my kidney and my bladder. To me, it just looked like lint on the X-ray, so I asked if he was sure. He just stared at me. "Yes, and it's as large as a raisin."

Suddenly, I felt really old.

As he proceeded to describe my options for removing the stone, I felt like King David having to choose his method of divine punishment after his impetuous census (see 2 Sam. 24:13–14). *None* of the options sounded good. I decided, as David had, that rather than placing myself in the hands of man I would fall upon the mercies of God—and see if the stone would pass on its own.

As it turned out, God's mercies took their sweet time.

Dealing with chronic pain day after day, sometimes minute by minute, can challenge a belief in the goodness of God. Waiting for that little darling to pass made me rethink my theology of purgatory. After three weeks, the little monster was finally exorcised from my body.

"You need to drink more water," the doctor urged me on my follow-up visit. Um, *yes*—I was convinced. *Converted* might be a better word. You see, the kidney stone wasn't my problem. It only revealed it. My problem was dehydration.

Sometimes the pain we experience—be it physical, emotional, or spiritual—just comes as part of living in a fallen world. But very often, God allows painful tests in our lives to serve as a warning that something needs to change. Usually that *something* is us.

In these moments of painful revelation, God is waiting on us.

As the brothers summited the hill country at Hebron, they saw their home in the distance and their father, Jacob—with Benjamin an arm's length away. As the old man craned his neck to see his sons, his heart sank.

Once again, a son was missing.

The nine remaining brothers explained about the Egyptian lord who took them for spies. They described how he had kept Simeon imprisoned as collateral and demanded they return with Benjamin to prove they were honest men. The prime minister's message was clear: if Benjamin didn't come to Egypt, they would never see Simeon again—and they could have no more grain. Then they sheepishly added that somehow their money had ended up back in their sacks. In other words, they *had* to return to Egypt or live as thieves. *Great.*

Jacob's response came like the bursting of a dam: "You have bereaved me of my children: Joseph is no more, and Simeon is no more, and you would take Benjamin; all these things are against me" (Gen. 42:36).

Did you catch that? "Simeon is no more." In other words, Simeon is as good as gone—because Benjamin *ain't* going to Egypt. The insinuation Jacob had given when the brothers left for Egypt the first time now proved blatantly obvious: Benjamin was important, and the rest of his sons were expendable.

Welcome home, guys.

Reuben stepped up and, as he had tried to do before by rescuing Joseph from death, offered to bring Benjamin home safely from the journey. Reuben even put up the lives of his own two sons as security. But no deal. From Jacob's perspective, every time these brothers had come home, they had brought him bad news of a lost son. No way would he risk losing Benjamin! Better to live as a thief. Better to live without Simeon. Better to take a chance on the famine. "All these things are against me," Jacob said. But were they really?

Exactly what role did God play in Jacob's mind?

<hr />

Years ago one of my daughters, as a toddler, came to me and said, "In the air, Daddy, in the air!"[1] She wanted me to toss her in the air and catch her. So I did, to her utter delight. My other daughter saw this and asked me to toss her too. Yet as she leveled off, her face twisted into sheer terror. When I caught her, she clung to me with all four limbs and begged, "No, Daddy—not again!"

Later I considered why the same flight gave joy to one and terror to the other. I think one focused on my ability to catch her, and the other obsessed on her inability to control the flight.

As my daughters have now become young women, I find myself in a similar situation. I still see them being hurled into the air, but instead of me doing the tossing and catching, God the Father flings them—while I helplessly watch from a distance. In those moments I become acutely aware of the struggle between my confidence in God's ability versus my own.

Every parent faces this tension. We want our children to follow God, but we also struggle to let God lead them. And so the very love that wants the best for them becomes the barrier that keeps them from receiving it. Only God knows what's truly best, and his will often includes journeys to Egypt that require our children to develop their faith apart from us—so that God becomes *their* God and not just ours.

We can hold nothing—not even a child—more dearly than our trust in God. If we truly trust God's providence, we will rest in the assurance that our sons and daughters remain as safe in harm's way as in their beds at home. On the other hand, if the Father calls them home to heaven ahead of us, we cannot prevent such circumstances by providing any amount of protection. We will seldom experience the peace we seek from God without surrendering to God what we pray for. Ultimately, our comfort about our children cannot come from the assurance that God will protect them, ironic as that sounds. Our comfort comes when we trust the Lord who remains in complete control and who will accomplish his good purposes, even in the worst circumstances. That cannot change, even when evil appears to have won the day.

I confess these principles come easier to write than to do. As I watch God toss my daughters in the air, I tend to focus on my inability to control the flight instead of God's ability to catch them. In this I find the gnawing conviction that I would rather feel in control than trust God to guard and guide the future of my children. Such is the challenge of all believing parents.

Our love for our children grows to resemble the Lord's love for them only when we allow him to lead them as he chooses. God waits for us to surrender. As we do, we bow not in an admission of defeat but in an act of worship.

Jacob faced a similar test with his children. But this wasn't the first time he faced it. Three decades earlier, he had placed his favorite son, Joseph, behind the other brothers as protection from a danger he feared would befall them—but didn't. That same scene found Jacob wrestling with God by the Jabbok River for control of his life. And before God could bless Jacob, he had to cripple him—and then wait on his response. The pain finally pulled from the patriarch a prayer for blessing. God gave it. Lesson learned.

But not really.

As it turned out, Jacob's wrestling match at the Jabbok lasted much longer than the sunrise. Thousands of daybreaks would appear before Jacob would let go of the fight to control his life. God would have to wrench from Jacob everything from his hip to his favorite wife to his sons to the potential loss of his whole family before he would surrender to God.

Now, thirty years later, Jacob found himself still wrestling. He still had his favorite son behind the other brothers. But now, his name was Benjamin.

The blending of two truths about faith leads to a principle that applies them both. Because the righteous person lives by faith (see Hab. 2:4), and because faith is the conviction of things not seen (see Heb. 11:1), God may test us with situations that seem to contradict what we believe.

Jacob's scenario reminds me of the test God gave his grandfather Abraham: "Take now your son, your only son, whom you love, Isaac, and go to the land of Moriah, and offer him there" (Gen. 22:2). Jacob knew the story of the binding of Isaac. His father—Isaac—had told him. But how could Isaac have ever told him if he had died on Mount Moriah? Jacob's very existence owed itself to the fact that God honored Abraham's willingness to surrender to God the son he loved. Could the Lord not accomplish the same thing for Jacob after he surrendered Benjamin?

For Abraham, sacrificing his son required more faith than did the twenty-five years of waiting for God's promise of Isaac. That's a good lesson to remember as we wait on God. God sometimes requires more from us after he gives us what we waited for. Specifically, he often waits for us to be willing to give it back. Suppose we ask God for a spouse. If God says yes, are we willing to give our spouse back to God? What if the Father opens the door to our dream job? Are we willing to walk away should God require it? Or suppose we ask the Lord for a baby. Are we also willing to give that child back to God?

Abraham was. Jacob wasn't. From Jacob's perspective, his sons were *his* sons.

Abraham had passed the test in three days. But so far, God had waited on Jacob for three decades. In fact, the whole narrative skids to a halt until Jacob surrenders Benjamin to God. And God is immeasurably patient. After all, he makes stalactites drop by drop. He has made lots of them.

Each parched day of the famine followed another until finally the grain sacks hung limp. Jacob told his boys to return to Egypt and buy for them just "a little food" (43:2). Surely just a little would be okay?

Judah stepped forward with the voice of reason. He may have remembered the futility of his own fear that had kept him from surrendering his son to Tamar and preserving his tribe's line. God's providence had proved to Judah the senselessness of resisting God's will. Now Judah saw that same timidity in his father. Judah reminded Jacob that Benjamin alone was their meal ticket. They could not return to the Egyptian lord without Benjamin. Judah then reiterated the offer Reuben proposed and promised to take personal responsibility for Benjamin's safety. Then he added, "For if we had not delayed, surely by now we could have returned twice" (v. 10). Two round trips from Hebron to Egypt amounted to roughly nine hundred miles—or seven weeks of hard travel. Jacob's reluctance to comply had wasted almost two months, and he only found himself facing the same issue all over again.

Finally, Jacob surrendered. At last, God's waiting on Jacob had paid off.

"If it must be," he conceded, "take your brother also and go back to the man at once. . . . As for me, if I am bereaved, I am bereaved" (vv. 11, 13–14 NIV). God's sovereign orchestration of events wrenched Benjamin from Jacob's arms and forced him to do what he would never do otherwise: trust God with his sons.

Sometimes that's the only way we learn.

I always get a kick out of the road tests automakers perform on one another. As objective as the tests claim to be, the goals remain clear. GM tests Ford to show Ford's weaknesses. GM tests GM to show its strengths. When Ford does the testing, however, the purpose completely reverses. Actually, this type of testing is biblical. Both God and Satan perform tests on us. These tests reveal how the rubber meets the road in our Christian lives. But the two tests have two completely different goals.

When we read the New Testament, we see in the original language two words for *test* we can easily mistake for synonyms. One word (*dokimazo*) has as its goal *a test for the purpose of approval*. Another word (*peirazo*) has as its goal, generally speaking, *a test to show weakness or a point of failure*.

Whenever Satan "tests" us, the word is always *peirazo*—that is, the goal of his test is to entice us to sin. Hence the test often gets appropriately translated as "temptation." A simple example finds its warning in relation to the frequency of marital intimacy: "Stop depriving one another, except by agreement for a time, so that you may devote yourselves to prayer, and come together again so that Satan will not tempt you [*peirazo*] because of your lack of self-control" (1 Cor. 7:5).

Satan has one goal in temptation: our failure.

On the other hand, we never find God tempting us—or placing us in a situation where our failure is his goal. James makes this clear: "Let no one say when he is tempted, 'I am being tempted [*peirazo*] by God'; for God cannot be tempted by evil, and He Himself does not tempt [*peirazo*] anyone" (James 1:13). Sometimes the testing of God occurs to discover the good or evil in our hearts, but never with the goal of enticing us to evil (see Heb. 11:17). God's tests have our approval as their goal. This remains true even after we die.

> Now if any man builds on the foundation with gold, silver, precious stones, wood, hay, straw, each man's work will become evident; for the day will show it because it is to be revealed with fire, and the fire itself will test [*dokimazo*] the quality of each man's work. (1 Cor. 3:12–13)

The foundation, in context, is Jesus Christ. God's "testing" of us at the judgment seat of Christ will find its basis in the quality and motive of the lives we build on that foundation (see 1 Cor. 4:5).

The goal of this test is our approval.

Thankfully, even when we face Satan's temptation designed to entice us to fail, God steps in to provide help. Consider this familiar verse and its promise:

> No temptation [that has as its goal your failure] has overtaken you but such as is common to man; and God is faithful, who will not allow you to be tempted beyond what you are able, but with the temptation will provide the way of escape also, so that you will be able to endure it. (1 Cor. 10:13)

Every single time Satan tempts us to sin, God steps in to provide a way of escape. Sin then, for the Christian, becomes a choice—not a compulsion.

Sometimes, admittedly, it's tough to discern the difference between a test and a temptation. But whether the test we face represents Satan tempting us to fail or God testing us to succeed, our response to the situation should always—always—remain the same.

We should obey God.

The Lord has a lot of dog food stores, have you noticed? He meets us there to reveal the blind spots we have that keep us from growing.

I'll be honest; in these moments of painful self-revelation I have often felt helpless, because the sins God exposed were kneejerk reactions. Sins I deliberately commit, I can also intentionally *not* commit. But involuntary sins stay with me like stink on a skunk. Any change I attempt feels like trying to change the shape of my nose. I push and push, but it snaps right back. I cannot change myself. Only God can.

There's an important distinction between becoming a weaker person and becoming more aware of one's weaknesses. One is regression and the other maturation. If we could uncover the manhole over our hearts and look inside, we'd see a tar pit a mile deep. Of course, it's too uncomfortable to do that, so we keep the lid on tight. But the Lord reveals our blind spots anyway—not to shame us but to give us an appreciation for his grace. How? By helping us realize he sees our mile-deep tar pit—as well as the other ten miles below it we can't see. He sees the raw, ugly parts of our hearts we never knew to look for, and yet he loves us anyway. When he meets us in these places of our weakness, he brings his grace along.

Because Jesus Christ died for our sins and rose again, his grace reverses our focus when we come face-to-face with our sin. Instead of coiling in a fetal position of shame, we grow to realize the depth of his love and the extent of his grace. God's grace makes it safe for us to see ourselves because we know that, regardless of what we find, God will never reject us. When he looks at us, he sees the righteousness of his holy Son, Jesus—all our weaknesses notwithstanding.

God honored Jacob's dogged determination to receive a blessing only after a displaced hip wrenched a prayer from the patriarch. It took pain. Hosea would later record Jacob's wrestling match as an example of weeping as well as prevailing (see Hosea 12:4)—that is, of weakness as well as strength. This paradox, which Jacob illustrates and Hosea applies, finds its fullest explanation in Paul's confession: "When I am weak, then I am strong" (2 Cor. 12:10). Jacob wrestled with tears but ultimately prevailed by confessing his need for God's blessing. Paul prayed three times for the Lord to remove the thorn in his flesh but finally rejoiced at the perspective his weakness gave him: God's grace is sufficient.

Wrestling with God always reveals our weaknesses, and thus, our dependence on him (see 2 Cor. 1:9–10). The Lord leaves tangible reminders of this principle in our lives for those days we forget about it. For Jacob, it was a limp, and for Paul, a thorn.

Each of our lives has its limps and thorns, but sadly, we can forget the connection between our weakness and God's strength. In fact, sometimes we can go so far as to turn a blind eye to sins that used to be mere blind spots. But because God loves us, he refuses to allow us to avoid reality.

"The hard facts of life, which knock some of the nonsense out of us," Derek Kidner writes, "are God's facts and His appointed school of character; they are not alternatives to His grace, but a means of it."[2] When we refuse to trust and obey God, he waits for us to do so by allowing circumstances to compel us.

As a result, God's will for our lives seldom follows a smooth path.

Years earlier, Jacob's barren wife Rachel issued him a ludicrous demand: "Give me children, or else I die" (Gen. 30:1). Exactly what was Jacob supposed to do differently? Sometimes we demand of people—or silently expect from them—what only God can provide.

God withholds, so we make demands of those whom we see as the channel. Jacob's response was accurate: "Am I in the place of God?" (v. 2). Jacob pointed to God's sovereignty as the reason for her barrenness. Ironically, after God did grant Rachel her second son, she died anyway. Then the pendulum of fear swung to Jacob's heart. He clung to Joseph and Benjamin as to his own life.

Rachel demanded to have children, and Jacob demanded to keep them. Was there really any difference between her insistence and his stubbornness?

From the perspective of Jacob and his sons, the famine was the problem. But it really wasn't.

From God's perspective, the famine merely revealed two bigger problems: Jacob's refusal to trust God and the brothers' jealous and treacherous attitudes. God used the famine to drag his rake across their hard hearts and unearth sins these men had kept buried far too long. Without the famine, Jacob never would have surrendered Benjamin and the brothers never would have done what we'll see in the next chapter.

God's method hasn't changed. This type of wrenching experience does more than hurt us. It frees us from the past where our fears have fenced us off from our potential. These arduous events compel us to follow the Lord out the gate and into the broad, open field of his unknown will. Following God is not an escape from pain but a preparation through pain for a future made greater by it. Joseph made this connection, and so must we.

We define our doctrine as theists, but too often we live our lives as functional deists. In other words, our doctrinal statements confess God as sovereign and involved in our lives, but in the real world we live as though we believe he's not involved enough. In these long gaps of life, waiting on God feels like waiting for a tree to grow. And because he just sits there while life passes us by, we try to push, manipulate, and cut corners to get results.

Like Jacob, we see the famine as the problem. God sees the famine as the revealer of our problem. In many cases, when we find ourselves asking God to change our circumstances, the reality is that God intends to use our circumstances to change us. He is the initiator, remember, and he waits for us to respond.

When we try to escape the struggle God has us in, we only run to another struggle. The brothers sold Joseph only to have him replaced by Benjamin. When we run, God merely changes his agent of change. Any other situation we chase will only reveal the same weakness in our hearts.

That jerk at the office, for example, isn't my real problem. Nor is my debt my problem. Nor my marriage. Or my neighbor's polka music. These just reveal my problem.

Me. I'm my problem.

The same is true with your office, your debt, your marriage, and your neighbor. Your heart is revealed in your office and in your marriage because that's where *you* are. Any other place and you'd still be asking for a transfer. But you can't transfer out of you.

Thankfully, neither are we stuck. God really does offer change.

A couple of months ago I noticed the "maintenance" light come on in my car. That meant the oil and filter needed changing. I thought, *Yeah, I'll do that soon.* Right. About a month went by and I thought, *You know, I really need to deal with that.* I forgot again. It wasn't until a couple weeks later I finally got them changed. I put it off because I'm a busy guy—and hey, oil and filters can always wait another day.

But then another warning light went on. This one was urgent. An exclamation point lit up my tire pressure light. When that warning goes off—or worse, when I have a flat tire—I immediately stop and deal with it. I have to or I don't move forward. Flats don't roll. And blowouts can kill.

That got me to thinking how our lives are like both filters and flats. But mostly like filters. We can disregard most warning lights in our lives for a while. In fact, they can blink so often we come to see them as normal—and we ignore them. Then one day that area of our life shuts down as our spouse makes a surprising confession, or our son or daughter rebels, or the doctor's report brings grim news.

We know the warnings are real—but we assume there will always be another day to deal with the issue. (There always has been.) In fact, we fully intend to deal with it. Seriously, we will deal with it. Someday.

There's a reason God waits for us. The reason connects to his kindness. I like how Joe Dallas puts it:

> God gives you room to take care of the problem before the problem overwhelms you. If you've been given space to repent, you'll do one of two things: you'll either use it wisely by taking action while you can, or you'll make the common mistake of mistaking space for repentance as permission to continue. That's easy to do, because we tend to be consequence-driven. When we get away with something once, we're inclined to think we'll get away with it indefinitely.[3]

God includes warning lights in his Word as well as in the dashboards of our guilty consciences. As they appear, we easily can ignore them. But we can't afford to disregard them. Blowouts stop everything.

With that in mind, let me toss you a few questions. Is there some specific area where Jesus has been knocking at the door, but you keep it dead-bolted? Is there something God is asking you to release to him that you're refusing to let go of? Some act of obedience where trusting God seems too much to ask? Some dream or desire that's so strong it overshadows what might be the Lord's desire for you? Are you afraid that God's will may not be your will—or that

151

somehow what he wants for you pales in comparison to what you want? These aren't rhetorical questions, by the way.

Take a moment now, as you're reading this chapter, and think with me. Think of just one warning light you see in your life you have habitually ignored. Got it in your mind? Imagine how you would feel if the worst possible news occurred in this area. Think through the fallout that would follow. Don't be afraid of the specifics. Say the bad news out loud. How would you *feel*?

One truth we all would feel, if we failed in this way, would be a longing to return and have a second chance. Through the gift of perspective, we have that chance today.

Choose a day and time—right now—when you will address the issue, make the phone call, or begin a new pattern. Explain to a friend why this is important to you, and then ask that friend to hold you accountable.

Honestly, you really can't afford to stay as you are. None of us can continually disregard God's warnings. They come because he loves us.

Have you noticed you always have something to trust God for in your life? The Father often uses outward and painful experiences to sharpen our inner sensitivity to his voice. God may awaken us to our need for his mercy by giving us a little taste of justice. He may allow fiery trials to melt the wax from our ears so that we can finally hear what he told us all along. He waits on us to respond and to follow him courageously. God is waiting for us in these painful places.

We can sum up our assignment in any circumstance with two words and a song: trust and obey. Nowhere does God say we have to understand our situation or his sovereign will. Just trust and obey.

God is waiting.

When God waits, however, he doesn't stand like a parent with arms folded, tapping a foot and glaring at us. Instead, he waits with arms outstretched. His waiting is an invitation. The gap of time in which God waits reflects his grace. As Paul wrote, "Do you think lightly of the riches of His kindness and tolerance and patience, not knowing that the kindness of God leads you to repentance?" (Rom. 2:4). He stands at the door and knocks—and waits.

He takes the initiative, and then he waits for us to respond and to repent. *That is the change he offers.* At least, that's where it must begin.

Consider the joy you would have if you surrendered the life you want and instead embraced the life God is waiting to give you.

The morning sun cut deep shadows across the hill country as Judah and his brothers took Benjamin, loaded their donkeys, and bid goodbye to a weepy old man. Before they departed, Jacob raised his feeble arms and blessed them: "May God Almighty grant you compassion in the sight of the man, so that he will release to you your other brother and Benjamin. And as for me, if I am bereaved of my children, I am bereaved" (Gen. 43:14).

As the brothers pointed their donkeys southwest toward the Negev, which led to "The Way of Shur" and to Egypt, Jacob leaned on his staff, gimped forward, and squinted.

Through a blur of tears, he watched his sons—especially Benjamin—until they had descended into the trees and finally were out of sight.

Benjamin was gone.

As Jacob turned to make his way home he faced north, where years ago he had sent Joseph to find his brothers—along the very same road.

Now, all of his sons—*gone.*

The brothers heaved a sigh of relief. To them this trip meant food for the famine. That's it. But over these many years, the Lord had prepared them for something more.

For something *far* greater.

For *forgiveness.*

8

A LONG RESOLUTION

How shall I go up to my father if the lad is not with me?

Genesis 44:34

Early Thanksgiving morning in 2003, Cathy answered our phone only to stare in silence for a full half-minute. Her quiet gaze slowly turned my direction.

"What is it?" I mouthed. She covered the phone.

"Wayne, it's the worst possible news about your mother."

One hour later found us shivering in our van outside my mom's mobile home, waiting for the coroner to examine the shell of the woman who had given birth to me thirty-six years earlier. As it turned out, Mom had died alone, two days prior, from what the medical report would deem an accidental mix of prescription sleeping pills and alcohol. The night before Thanksgiving, my sister had intended to drive up and stay with Mom, but a flat tire delayed the trip. If not for the flat, my sister would have found Mom that night, as opposed to someone else finding her the next morning. Sometimes these delays—these flat tires, these red lights, these gaps—represent God's mercy.

My parents divorced before my first birthday, and my nomadic childhood saw Mom marry two more times, each ending in divorce. She would have wed even again if she could have—and then some. "I don't care how many times I have to get married," Mom told me one day, "I'm going to *find* a man who will make me happy." I once saw a witty picture of a female skeleton slumped on a park bench holding a dog skeleton. Cobwebs covered her dress, hat, and handbag. The caption read: "Waiting for the Perfect Man." Mom told me a joke once that reminded me of that picture. The perfect man and the perfect woman are driving in a car. As they pass through an intersection, they crash into Santa Claus. Who survives the collision, the perfect man, the perfect woman, or Santa Claus? Answer: the perfect woman, because the other two don't exist!

My mother was a beautiful woman. Actually, *stunning* seems a better word. As I grew up, boys in the neighborhood would say to me, "Whoa, *that's* your mother? She's hot!" That usually earned them a slug. Mothers aren't supposed to be hot. They're supposed to be available and nurturing. They're supposed to become grandmothers and great-grandmothers. But they're not supposed to die at age fifty-six. As Mom aged, even her beauty couldn't escape the inevitable effects of time. And as her years increased, so did her desperation to find a man to make her happy. Standards slid. Time grew short.

Far shorter, in fact, than anyone imagined.

Mom's tragic death shocked me because my prayers had a different goal. For years I had clung to a verse that taught me I always "ought to pray and not to lose heart" (Luke 18:1). I prayed God would help Mom release her dependence on alcohol and relationships and turn instead to the Lord for help—and then disciple and counsel other women.

For whatever reason, a sovereign God said no.

He took her home instead.

As I waited outside Mom's trailer that Thanksgiving morning, the "what-ifs" flooded my mind. What if my parents had remained married? What if my mother had sought solace in God rather than in booze? What if I had been more involved in her life? What if I had prayed harder? What if . . .

But I've discovered that entering the "what-ifs" room gives a person nowhere to stand. That kind of thinking comes to nothing, like searching for a flicker of light in a yawning black cavern. What-ifs only intensify grief and invite blame-shifting.

The sight of the medical examiner rolling away my mom in a body bag will remain forever fixed in this little boy's heart. I missed my mother. I still miss her.

Even though I felt hurt that God said no to my prayers, I also experienced great relief. I praised God that Mom had trusted in Jesus years earlier. I thanked him that no man would ever violate her again and that she was finally free of her burden of living. Plus, she had finally found what she was looking for—a man who would make her happy. She now sees Jesus in person.

Now she waits no longer.

As you can imagine, I've shared only the tip of the iceberg. In a fallen world, we all have our dysfunctional stories that lurk under the surface of the waves. You have your own icebergs, just as I have mine (as do our kids, by the way). As we grow and make our way through life, we do our best to steer clear of these bergs that threaten to rip holes in our hulls and send us to the bottom. Sometimes we cope with life's disappointments by masking the pain, or by searching for something or someone to make us happy, but these never work out because our icebergs never float away on their own.

Only God can show us how to deal with them—and amazingly, to see them as part of his plan.

Jacob didn't see this yet. He only saw his sons leaving again—especially Benjamin.

The twelve-day journey from Canaan to Egypt opened a whole new world for Benjamin, the baby of the family. The hill country surrounding Hebron, with its valleys, trees, and cool evening breezes, slowly sloped down into the warm Negev and the long, flat, desert road that lay beyond it. The trip afforded Benjamin his first taste of freedom ever, with every turn of his head providing sights Jacob's youngest son had never seen before.

As the sun set in the brothers' faces the final day of their trip, they dismounted and set up camp in anticipation for the morning.

And oh, what the next two days would hold!

Sunup found the brothers saddled and loaded, trotting their donkeys into the city and requesting an audience with Joseph. As they faced the powerful vicegerent of Egypt once again, still unaware of his identity, Benjamin now stood beside them. They had brought their younger brother as Joseph had requested.

But instead of giving them grain and dismissing them for home, Joseph turned and muttered in Egyptian to his house steward—then left. The steward ushered the brothers out of the public eye and directed them to Joseph's private residence.

This struck fear in the brothers' hearts: "It is because of the money that was returned in our sacks the first time that we are being brought in," they said, "that he may seek occasion against us and fall upon us, and take us for slaves with our donkeys" (Gen. 43:18). When the brothers had discovered their returned money on the first trip home from Egypt, they interpreted the money as God intervening because of what they had done to Joseph (see 42:28). It served as part of the Lord's awakening of their consciences. If the subsequent weeks in Canaan had scabbed the old wound the previous visit had reopened, the steward's response must have opened it again: "Your God and the God of your father has given you treasure in your sacks; I had your money" (43:23). The statement would have seemed both comforting and disconcerting.

God clearly had his hand in these events.

Remember Simeon? If the brothers' consciences had quieted over the last few weeks, Simeon's had only intensified in volume. By the time the brothers returned to Egypt, Simeon had sat in prison for more than two months—when he expected to do so for only several weeks. Simeon could count. He had traveled down to Egypt; he knew if they had hurried they could have returned twice by now. He must have figured his brothers had abandoned him and he was getting what he deserved for abandoning Joseph. Just as Joseph had expected a speedy release from prison after the cupbearer's freedom—but instead had waited another two years—so Simeon had to wait on God for two months. But Simeon's prison door finally opened, and the steward brought him out to his brothers. It must have been a wonderful reunion.

But it was nothing compared to the reunion that would happen shortly.

The gaps in the Bible's narratives omit scores of details we'd love to know about dozens of issues. On other topics though, remarkably, it seems just the opposite. Scripture supplies *liberal* space for minutiae that seem altogether trivial.

Take genealogies, for example. Do we really need nine chapters of 1 Chronicles to tell us who begat whom? I mean, would our faith fall apart if we didn't know Hadad begat Bedad? And what about Deuteronomy's lengthy retelling of the Law? Or even the huge amount of content devoted to Peter's visit to Cornelius—and then its detailed repetition in the chapter that follows? These represent only samples of what seem like lopsided emphases on the irrelevant. Hey, if we can only have so many verses in the Bible, could we not give a little less space to the genealogies and more to, say, how to parent a teenager? To us, it makes little sense.

If you've ever studied a foreign language, you may have wondered why it doesn't just keep things simple and work the way English does. After all, English makes much more sense. It just seems *right*. Our familiarity with our native language—whatever the language—makes it seem best. Even though our problem lies with our ignorance of the quirks of an unfamiliar language's grammar, syntax, and vocabulary, we still can't shake the feeling that it's the *language* that's the problem—not us. Strange how we think that, isn't it? Most of the significant learning we glean in life begins with us scratching our heads.

So, of course, our most significant study—God's Word—often finds us scratching. We learn by scratching. We'll struggle to grasp the quirks of God's lopsided emphases when our way of thinking makes so much more sense. Eventually we discover that our questions about the purpose of genealogies and Deuteronomy and Cornelius all have answers—good ones. Even our deeper questions about God and life and suffering (and teenagers) have answers, but we may lack the capacity to understand them. The finite cannot grasp the infinite.

God reveals what he wants us to know, what we need to know, and what we can apply—but not all at once. Sometimes we wait on God for the answers. Sometimes he waits on us until we choose to hear them. And yet, even with all the gaps the Bible has, the small slice of the infinite that represents the Bible's divine revelation requires a lifetime of study. In spite of all it leaves out, the Word of God still remains an inexhaustible text. A lifetime of head scratching only scratches the surface of what the Bible offers.

Biblical gaps prove that God realizes the value of word count. He has wasted no space. So when the text includes copious details on some trivial subject or event, we know God has underlined it as important—regardless of whether or not it seems relevant to us just yet.

That's what we see with Joseph's story as the sun set on the final day of the brothers' second journey to Egypt. Genesis gives most of chapter 43, as well as all of chapter 44 and the majority of chapter 45, to describe the unfolding events of only two days. But really, it's only about twenty-four hours, from morning to morning.

Genesis devotes more text to these twenty-four hours than to any other days in the book. That ought to raise a flag in our minds. Moreover, as we observe the chiasm that represents the whole Joseph story from Genesis 37–50, a flare ought to fire in our brains. (Remember, as we saw in chapter 4, a chiasm represents an intentional structural arrangement in which the text reveals an emphasis.) The chiasm of the entire Joseph story culminates at this point.[1]

All that space—for about twenty-four hours. Why?

Because these twenty-four hours climax the past twenty-two years of Joseph waiting on God.

Joseph's brothers entered his home, and the steward informed them his master would have lunch with them at noon. (Likely, Asenath and the boys had stepped out for the day.) The brothers prepared the gifts they had brought—and then waited.

When Joseph came home, they presented him with their gifts—which offered tastes from his childhood: "a little balm and a little honey, aromatic gum and myrrh, pistachio nuts and almonds" (43:11). But Joseph said nothing of the presents. Instead, he inquired about them and about their father's welfare. He approached Benjamin, the only other son of his mother. The last time Joseph saw Benjamin, his baby brother was a mere ten years old. Now Benjamin stood before him a thirty-two-year-old man. No wonder Joseph had to ask, "Is this your youngest brother?" Then, at risk of

LETTING GO

breaking character, Joseph told Benjamin, "May God be gracious to you, my son" (v. 29). Deeply moved over seeing his brother—but unable to embrace him—Joseph rushed from the room and went to his private chamber to weep. Years of suffering and separation had failed to remove his love for his brother. Nor had the years of success and power hardened his heart.

When the brothers had departed from their father almost two weeks ago, Jacob had spoken a benediction over the boys: "May God Almighty grant you compassion in the sight of the man" (v. 14). The Hebrew term for *compassion* shares the same root as Joseph's reaction upon seeing Benjamin: he was "deeply" stirred. God was answering Jacob's prayer of benediction, a foreshadowing of how he would answer the rest of the prayer.

After washing his face, Joseph returned to the room and kept his composure. As much as he longed for reconciliation with them, Joseph had learned to wait on God's timing. The brothers still needed testing to see if they had changed—or if they would be willing to change. Sure, they had returned the money. But their father had told them to. How would they respond when only God did the prompting?

God would test them further—through the wise arrangements of Joseph's plan.

To further underscore God's involvement in the scene, Joseph had them seated for lunch according to their age—Reuben first, all the way down to Benjamin, in order of birth. The brothers' jaws dropped, and it wasn't for the meal. Clearly God had a hand in their circumstances. This arrangement would have done more than amaze these men; it would have spotlighted the missing son between Zebulun and Benjamin. At that moment, the family elephant would have squeezed in at the table where Joseph should have sat. The reek from its presence seemed inescapable.

Joseph served food to the brothers from his own table. And after each brother had received a portion, Joseph brought Benjamin more food, and then more food, and again more, and then more—five times as much as the other brothers!

The favorite son received special treatment—and without the protection of the doting father. Sound familiar? This echoed the situation they had found themselves in twenty-two years earlier when they stripped Joseph of his multicolored coat and got shed of him. Daddy wasn't around to protect him then, and Daddy wasn't here to protect Benjamin now.

Sitting downwind of nepotism can stink, and Joseph's brothers sniffed it again. How would they respond this time to the favorite son getting special treatment?

Other people's lives always seem better. Have you noticed? Even their struggles seem better! We stew over someone else's abilities, salaries, or bodies. We feel rejected when they get affirmed in front of us. When we compare ourselves with others, our kneejerk reaction is envy, discouragement, depression—or worse, pride. As Paul wrote, "When they measure themselves by themselves and compare themselves with themselves, they are not wise" (2 Cor. 10:12 NIV). Though we would deny it if asked, we often feel another person's success represents our failure. If we only had *their* conditions, our life would be so much better.

After Jesus told Peter how he would die, Peter went on to ask Jesus how *John* would die. (Don't you just love Peter?) "What is that to you?" Jesus answered him, "*You* follow Me!" (John 21:22; the original language has that emphasis). Jesus's answer remains a helpful reminder to us as well when we compare our sorry lot in life with those other Christians who have somehow sidestepped the icebergs. *What is that to you?* Jesus asks. The truth is, when comparing icebergs, all we ever see are the tips. Every one of us has more dysfunction hiding below the surface.

Our sovereign God chose each believer, before the foundation of the world, to be made anew by the same means—by grace through faith in Jesus Christ. Yet even with this common redemption, each of us remains a unique individual created for a special purpose. God's plan to shape us into the image of his beloved Son includes a marvelous diversity in the body of Christ (see 1 Cor. 12:7). But even though the Lord made us unique, he also intends we work together to accomplish something much greater and more beautiful than we ever could on our own. When we view someone else's situation or abilities as a threat to ours, we miss the benefit God intended us to reap from *their uniqueness*. When we try to impersonate a gift we lack, we hold back from others the greatest benefit we can contribute to them—*our uniqueness*.

Because God does the dispensing, we can understand that being different just means *different*, not better or worse. God remains sovereign down to the last detail of our lives. A problem with our situation means a problem with God.

As we saw in chapter 4, sometime the gaps of insignificance we find ourselves in boil down to our craving something larger for which we aren't equipped—and which God, in his love, repeatedly refuses us. Part of waiting on God includes praising him that providence sometimes refuses to give us *more*—more money, more giftedness, more success, more popularity—if getting *more* would actually generate a spiritual vacuum in our hearts.

To think we lack something because God wants to keep us from our potential is to believe the serpent's lie from Eden. God's love and protection come just as much from what he keeps as from what he gives.

Joseph gave Benjamin a lot more—a sovereign God gave Benjamin more—and to their credit, instead of reacting jealously toward Benjamin, the brothers "feasted and drank freely with him" (Gen. 43:34). It looked as if they passed the test of jealousy—a test they had botched twenty-two years earlier in their hatred and envy of Joseph, the favored son.

Wouldn't it be great to reconcile with the brothers now, Joseph? Not yet. One test to go—the big one.

To prepare for the brothers' departure the next morning, Joseph told his house steward to put their money back in their sacks once again and to plant Joseph's silver chalice in Benjamin's sack. The steward complied.

At first light, the brothers took their loaded donkeys and, with much relief, left the city and headed east to Canaan. They had food for the famine. They had Simeon back. They had kept Benjamin safe. Mission accomplished.

Not so fast.

Joseph waited for them to leave the city and then sent his steward to chase after them. The brothers heard galloping behind them and turned to see armed servants and a very stern-looking steward who accused them of stealing his master's silver cup! "Why have you repaid evil for good?" the steward asked, even before the cloud of dust could settle (44:4). Dumbfounded, the brothers protested. After all, why would they earlier return the money only to steal a cup now? They had proven their honesty. They felt so confident of their innocence they vowed that the one with whom the steward found the cup would die. He agreed but chose instead only to make the guilty man a slave.

The brothers lost no time, and each lowered their grain sacks to the ground. Joseph's steward began rifling through the grain— starting with the oldest brother and working his way to Benjamin. Sack after sack verified their innocence—until the last one.

Benjamin's sack had the cup.

Mortified, the brothers felt the implications roll over them like a tidal wave. Benjamin would be made a slave.

Yes, *Benjamin*.

Only Benjamin.

Jacob's favorite boy.

The only son of Rachel left.

The brother of the brother they had betrayed.

The son Jacob refused to send for fear something might happen.

The brother Judah vowed to watch over or else to bear the blame before his father forever.

Benjamin.

The brothers tore their clothes in mourning, and the sound of ripping would have brought to mind Jacob's identical reaction upon hearing of Joseph's supposed fate (see 37:34). They could already hear their father's mournful screams. Suddenly, the steward's question took on a different meaning: "Why have you repaid evil for good?"

It was as if they had betrayed Joseph all over again.

The brothers rode back to the city as silent as the long shadows that stretched in front of them—never taking their eyes off the road beneath their donkeys.

They arrived again at Joseph's house to find him hotter than a hornet. They collapsed to the ground before him. "What is this deed that you have done?" Joseph asked. "Do you not know that such a man as I can indeed practice divination?" (44:15). To attempt to divine the future, Egyptian rulers would interpret omens by scrutinizing the way liquid refracted light in a silver cup. Of course, Joseph no more used the cup for divination than they would. The cup simply served as part of Joseph's Egyptian disguise, and its surprising presence in Benjamin's sack became another means of awakening their consciences. But God *had* given Joseph the ability to see the future. The brothers lying flat before him fulfilled those dreams, in part.

With the brothers prostrate, Judah raised his head and confessed their guilt. Even though innocent of the crime for which Joseph charged them, the brothers understood their deeper culpability: "God has found out the iniquity of your servants" (v. 16), a confession that stretched back to twenty-two years earlier. Judah told Joseph they all would become slaves to the great man.

Joseph refused. Only Benjamin would be a slave.

Then Joseph pulled out the linchpin with one more phrase: "But as for you, go up in peace to your father" (v. 17).

In peace . . .

Stab. Twist. Feel the pain.

Joseph knew those words would slice a nerve, one way or the other. "Go up in peace to your father." They would either see the offer as an opportunity to rid themselves of the favorite son again and return to their father with another lie (and one less brother in the way of their wrangling for supremacy). Or they would respond to the long-standing promptings of God on their consciences, and given the opportunity they would never bring that kind of pain upon their father again.

Which would they choose?

They all lay on their faces before Joseph, feeling the weight of his words.

Judah rose, perhaps as far as his knees, and offered an appeal. His words remain one of the most eloquent and tender pleas ever recorded in the history of literature.

As you read Judah's entreaty to Joseph, try to imagine Benjamin's terror as his first taste of freedom turned into enslavement. Try to picture what the brothers knew of how the news of Benjamin would affect their father. Imagine Judah's sense of responsibility. And especially try to feel Joseph's inner turmoil as Judah's poignant plea landed on a heart God had prepared for more than two decades for this moment. Read carefully Judah's words, straight from Scripture:

> Oh my lord, may your servant please speak a word in my lord's ears, and do not be angry with your servant; for you are equal to Pharaoh. My lord asked his servants, saying, "Have you a father

or a brother?" We said to my lord, "We have an old father and a little child of his old age. Now his brother is dead, so he alone is left of his mother, and his father loves him." Then you said to your servants, "Bring him down to me that I may set my eyes on him." But we said to my lord, "The lad cannot leave his father, for if he should leave his father, his father would die." You said to your servants, however, "Unless your youngest brother comes down with you, you will not see my face again." Thus it came about when we went up to your servant my father, we told him the words of my lord. Our father said, "Go back, buy us a little food." But we said, "We cannot go down. If our youngest brother is with us, then we will go down; for we cannot see the man's face unless our youngest brother is with us." Your servant my father said to us, "You know that my wife bore me two sons; and the one went out from me, and I said, 'Surely he is torn in pieces,' and I have not seen him since. If you take this one also from me, and harm befalls him, you will bring my gray hair down to Sheol in sorrow." Now, therefore, when I come to your servant my father, and the lad is not with us, since his life is bound up in the lad's life, when he sees that the lad is not with us, he will die. Thus your servants will bring the gray hair of your servant our father down to Sheol in sorrow. For your servant became surety for the lad to my father, saying, "If I do not bring him back to you, then let me bear the blame before my father forever." Now, therefore, please let your servant remain instead of the lad a slave to my lord, and let the lad go up with his brothers. For how shall I go up to my father if the lad is not with me—for fear that I see the evil that would overtake my father? (vv. 18–34)

This was Judah's finest hour.

This is not the same man who had blurted twenty-two years earlier, "What profit is it for us to kill our brother and cover up his blood? Come and let us sell him to the Ishmaelites" (37:26–27). Nor is this the self-centered guardian of his own welfare who kept his youngest son from his duty for fear harm would come to him. Nor is this the self-gratifying male who would hire a harlot on a whim and yet give a verdict to have his own daughter-in-law executed for the same activity.

No, Judah had changed. God had changed him.

No doubt with hot tears running down his cheeks, Judah pled to a man he didn't know on the basis of emotions any man could feel. The grief of an old man who would lose his precious son. The memory of a beloved wife who had died. The love for a younger brother who had no guilt in this whole ugly business. Judah knew he could never return to his father without the one whom he vowed to keep safe. Go up in peace to his father? He knew he never could.

Peace includes peace of mind, and no selfish interest could override Judah's integrity this time around. He knew that peace would come only through personal sacrifice. Peace always requires it.

I heard of a father who walked into a room to see his young son with his hand inside an expensive vase. The boy explained he had dropped a penny in the vase, and now his hand was stuck. The dad tried everything to free his son's hand, but it stayed wedged. Finally, the father grabbed a hammer to break the vase. "Wait, Daddy!" the frightened boy said. "Would it help if I let go of the penny?"

We smile at the mind of a naïve child, and yet we often cling to the same baffling priorities—no matter how old we get. We often find ourselves at the breaking point of something valuable because we refuse to release something trivial. We cling to our pennies and break our vases.

It sounds like a contradiction, but it's true. With no personal sacrifice, we'll have no personal satisfaction. This type of sacrifice has nothing to do with surrendering one's integrity or compromising God's rules of morality. That's not sacrifice; that's sin. Godly sacrifice recognizes the difference between pennies and vases. And when it comes to relationships, we have no peace or reconciliation without sacrifice.

For example, let's say you and a friend have had a falling out, and your ego keeps you stuck. You risk damaging something far more valuable by clinging to pride. Or let's say your marriage is struggling because your expectations aren't happening. That may require some sacrifice of expectations. (Remember "for better or for worse"?) Or let's say you have a passion for music but you also need to pay the bills and provide for your family. Will you sacrifice your dream until God opens the door—if he ever does?

Some of our problems require a willingness to surrender saving face and our personal preferences—and in some cases, our passions and dreams—for the wellbeing of relationships far more valuable. Even God had to sacrifice in order to have a peaceful relationship with us (see John 15:13; Rom. 5:1). That kind of sacrifice has no ulterior motive. That attitude gives relationships priority over the pennies of pride and self-interest that shatter lives.

Got your hand stuck in a vase? Let go.

That's what Judah did. He realized peace would happen only through personal sacrifice. Instead of asking for mercy for Benjamin, Judah pled to take his place as a slave. Rather than chafe against his father's weakness for a favorite son, Judah begged to replace beloved Benjamin—the complete opposite of Judah's evil actions with Joseph—and chose to give up his own freedom so that his father could live out the rest of his days in peace.

Judah appealed to Joseph on the basis of the very qualities he and his brothers had betrayed years before: sacrifice, love, selflessness, and grace.

Judah, representing all his brothers, showed himself a different man now.

They had changed. That changed everything.

Joseph's immediate reaction to Judah's plea would have left the brothers unsure of the verdict.

But it didn't look good.

In a burst of passion, Joseph screamed something in Egyptian, and suddenly every Egyptian withdrew from the room. Joseph and his brothers were alone.

Joseph then pulled his finger from the dike, and out surged the tears and emotions he had pent up for so many years. He wept loudly and openly. Suddenly, the bewilderment of the brothers shifted to terror as the first direct words this ruler spoke to them came out in their own Hebrew language.

ANEE YOSEF!—"I am Joseph!" Then he added, "Is my father still alive?" (Gen. 45:3).

It's a good thing they were already lying flat when Joseph yelled this.

God had primed their consciences for this very moment. They had come to understand that their sin against Joseph would not stay buried. They saw the events of the past two months as coming from the hand of God, climaxing with their imminent slavery. To make matters worse, the object of their guilty consciences now stood resurrected before their eyes, with the power to have them executed, let alone enslaved!

To say "his brothers could not answer him" puts it mildly (v. 3). They laid before him in abject terror. They likely assumed God had brought them to this moment of poetic justice to require of them their lives.

They knew they deserved it. They were guilty.

Here it comes.

But rather than enslave Judah, or incarcerate all the brothers, or lop off all their heads, Joseph would have removed his own headdress so they could more easily see past his Egyptian garb. He invited them to their feet and to come closer to see him better.

Joseph identified himself again and immediately acknowledged the deep secret they had tried to keep buried for so, so long: "I am your brother Joseph, whom you sold into Egypt" (v. 4). After acknowledging their sin—notice, he didn't discount it—he quickly comforted them and urged them to release the grief and guilt of their evil act.

> Now do not be grieved or angry with yourselves, because you sold me here, for God sent me before you to preserve life. For the famine has been in the land these two years, and there are still five years in which there will be neither plowing nor harvesting. God sent me before you to preserve for you a remnant in the earth, and to keep you alive by a great deliverance. Now, therefore, it was not you who sent me here, but God. (vv. 5–8)

Here we see the pattern of Joseph's life that has undergirded his entire being. Joseph kept God in the constant forefront of his mind. When Potiphar's wife tempted him, he spoke of God. When the cupbearer and baker spoke of their dreams, Joseph gave God credit. When Pharaoh needed Joseph to interpret, once again he pointed to God. And now, perhaps in the most telling of all Joseph's testimonies of the Almighty, he referred to God a total of five times in this passage as the reason why his brothers needed to release their guilt and grief over a deed they could never go back and undo.

God became for Joseph more than a moral compass to guide his decisions. Joseph had learned to *look at every event in life through the filter of God's sovereignty. Even the bad events.*

This may be the biggest lesson Joseph's life teaches us. God works through all things in our lives, including every human decision and tragedy, to bring about his good purposes for us and for his glory.

Yes, he uses *all things*—even that one thing you think is an exception. Honestly, he may use that one thing most of all in your life.

Joseph's story shows the keys of God's providence opening doors on every level. Whether God moved in the heart of a national leader, like Pharaoh, or he controlled natural catastrophes, like famines (we still call them "acts of God"), or he gave personal dreams to key individuals, God caused all things to work together for his good purposes. The Lord even used the brothers' lush pasture in Dothan, the valley's international highway, and the timely Ishmaelite caravan all as part of the means to get Joseph to Egypt, which preserved Judah's line and which sent Jesus to earth to die for our sins, rise again, and promise to return to rule over God's kingdom.

I like the words of Puritan John Flavel: "Some providences, like Hebrew letters, must be read backwards."[2] Joseph looked back and saw God's sovereign hand involved in all events—even the painful ones.

Because our decisions work in concert with God's sovereignty, we can easily confuse events as occurring purely from our own doing. We work, and so God provides money. We pray, and so God answers prayer. We do this, and so God does that. In other words, as odd as it sounds, we see God as the effect and ourselves as the cause.

But this error of thinking gets us nowhere when we find ourselves in situations where we can do *nothing*. Impossible circumstances convince us we are not the cause.

Remember, as Creator, God initiates and we respond. Waiting begins with God. In following God's will, we will often see no way out of our situation. In fact, humanly speaking, there may be no way out. In those frightful moments when we find ourselves feeling cornered, it's tempting to leave the straight and narrow to find a way of escape or a quick solution to our pain. We can come up with ten airtight reasons why sticking with God's Word will flop. After all, it's impossible.

That kind of thinking urged Joseph's great-grandmother Sarah to flat-out laugh at God's fantastic promise that she, an old, barren woman, would bear a child. The Lord's response to her remains a question we all should answer: "Is anything too difficult for the LORD?" (Gen. 18:14). Um, that would be negative.

Our limitations in no way limit God. They merely provide opportunities for him to reveal his power in our lives. Even death cannot thwart the good plans God has for us. We may have endured a miserable situation after years of hoping and praying and waiting on God (like my family did with my mom). But instead of God working a miracle and changing a life, he may choose to take the life. For a God who can raise the dead—and who will—death changes nothing and has no effect on his promises. (The next chapter shows us even more of this marvelous truth.)

We find impossible situations frustrating, sure, but God intends those unreasonable and often unbearable circumstances to encourage us for the next round. In other words, what we learn from God in one situation applies to all circumstances. When we see God provide financially, we relate that to our struggles with our kids. When God encourages us with a quick answered prayer for a friend, we relate that to the family member we've prayed for since childhood. We connect what we learn about God's faithfulness in one area to all other areas of life.

That's what Joseph did. God custom-built Joseph's refining fire, allowing gut-wrenching experiences like betrayal, kidnapping, homesickness, slavery, temptations, false accusation, chains, solitude, and years of waiting. Nevertheless, Joseph saw God's hand on him in Potiphar's house, in the Round House, and in Pharaoh's court. Joseph connected the dots and applied the truth to his situation with his brothers. God would fulfill Joseph's dreams in God's time.

We should drink deeply from what Jesus promised: "With people it is impossible, but not with God; for all things are possible with God" (Mark 10:27). If we really believe that, we will expectantly wait for God's power and apply yesterday's lessons to today's impossible situations. God's miracles *require* impossible contexts, and we won't experience the joy of his power if we keep running away from the pain faithfulness demands of us.

As our mortal minds struggle to follow the plans of our immortal God, we must remember God never asks us to figure out a solution to our impossible situations. Instead, he calls us to trust him. Why should we? Because he has no limitations as we do. If God asks impossible things of us, he plans to do the impossible for us—in his time. Our job is to wait on God for the long resolution.

Joseph waited twenty-two years to reconcile with his brothers. There's nothing like a period of waiting and futility to show that blessing, success, and goodness in our lives come only from God. Joseph figured that out.

Clearly, Joseph had forgiven his brothers.

Joseph embraced Benjamin and they wept on each other's necks. Then Joseph "kissed all his brothers and wept on them, and afterward his brothers talked with him" (Gen. 45:15). What a great verse. Don't you wish you could have heard their conversation? The brothers probably told Joseph about their children, and he may have even introduced them to his own sons, Manasseh and Ephraim, as well as to Asenath, his bride of nine years. I like to think each brother would have apologized while embracing Joseph, and he gently would have reaffirmed his love and forgiveness to each one. Of course, they asked Joseph the obvious question: "How in the world did you get to be ruler of Egypt?!" As Joseph recounted his painful story to them, I'm sure his pain caused them to hurt again—and Joseph, again, pointed them to God.

But we can only guess what they said. Their conversation remains one of the many gaps in Scripture we'll never fill in. When the Lord inspired Moses to record this scene, the Holy Spirit drew the curtain across the brothers' tender, private conversation. "Afterward his brothers talked with him." We can only imagine.

One thing we do know about this scene, however. Joseph had his chair back at the table. The family elephant no longer lingered. Forgiveness caused it to flee.

Gone.

There's no room for elephants in a room filled with grace.

When Pharaoh heard about Joseph's brothers coming, he told Joseph to give them what they needed to bring their father to Egypt. Joseph did so, providing the wagons and sustenance necessary to carry Jacob and all the brothers' households to Egypt.

I find it fascinating how Joseph waited on God for this long resolution with his brothers, but once the forgiveness had come between them, Joseph wasted no time in urging them to bring their father, Jacob, to Egypt (see 45:9, 13). Joseph recognized God's plan first required reconciliation with the brothers and then relocation of the whole family. The famine had begun two years ago, and they faced another five years of drought.

As the brothers departed for Canaan, Joseph reminded them of the obligation of grace: "Do not quarrel on the journey" (v. 24).

These parting words from Joseph served as more than a mere reminder to be nice. The ride home would give them twelve days to mull over the inevitable conversation they faced in Hebron. The good news about Joseph would come easy enough, as well as the promise of provision for the famine. But how would they admit to their father what they had done to Joseph so long ago? They couldn't serve Jacob another half-baked batch of lies. He would hear the truth from Joseph soon enough. The confession had to come.

Joseph knew the temptation would prove strong to rehearse their failures on the journey and to blame-shift their guilt to each other. After all, Reuben had tried to rescue Joseph, and Judah had suggested selling him instead of killing him. Joseph knew his brothers, and so he urged them to keep peace with each other as they rode home.

Jacob had watched his calendar. He knew when to expect his boys' return, and the old man would have stationed a lookout. As he received news that his sons approached Hebron, he must have dreaded what bad news he would discover this time. When he saw the large caravan of wagons that approached, he knew *something* had happened. Jacob craned his neck to count heads and rejoiced when he caught glimpse of Benjamin and Simeon and all the rest of his sons. No doubt a silent prayer of thanksgiving ascended from the old man.

But before Jacob could ask about all the wagons, his sons spoke words he never imagined he would hear: "Joseph is still alive, and indeed he is ruler over all the land of Egypt" (v. 26).

No response.

Jacob stood absolutely stunned.

Remember, when Jacob last saw his sons he had no clue if he would ever see them again. He had given up on Joseph a lifetime ago, and he reluctantly surrendered Benjamin to the request of the lord of Egypt. Jacob had steeled himself with the possibility of never seeing them again. Then this entourage rolls in, not only with Benjamin and Simeon and all the brothers but also with news of Joseph!

Understandably, the old man "was stunned," a phrase from a Hebrew term meaning limp or useless. He went numb.

Twenty-two years earlier, the rebellious brothers produced convincing evidence of Joseph's death, referring to him only as "your son" (37:32; see Luke 15:30). Now, however, the repentant brothers produced compelling evidence of Joseph's life—and they even called him by name: "Joseph is alive."

Then came the tough part. Their explanation had to include their confession. And although Moses records the conversation with discretion, we know it must have occurred in this moment. (Again, sometimes gaps in retelling experiences are gracious.)

When they told him all the words of Joseph that he had spoken to them, and when he saw the wagons that Joseph had sent to carry him, the spirit of their father Jacob revived. Then Israel said, "It is enough; my son Joseph is still alive. I will go and see him before I die." (45:27–28)

They wasted no time and packed for Egypt.

Their first day out brought them twenty miles southwest, as far as Beersheba. In years to come, Beersheba would come to represent the practical southern border of Israel, "from Dan to Beersheba" (Judg. 20:1), becoming the last stop before the wilderness. Throughout Scripture Beersheba served as a point of departure for many spiritual journeys. Abraham, Hagar, Jacob, and Elijah all experienced life-changing encounters with God in association with the site (see Gen. 16:8; 21:14–18; 46:1–5; 1 Kings 19:3).

But Beersheba would have held special memories for Jacob. The city received its name from his grandfather Abraham. Jacob's parents, Isaac and Rebekah, raised Jacob and his brother, Esau, at Beersheba. Most touching, perhaps, would be Jacob remembering the places of his youth and the last place he ever saw his mother, Rebekah, before he fled from Esau to his mother's hometown in Paddan-Aram. Just the day before, in Hebron, Jacob had left the burial site of his parents and grandparents at the cave of Machpelah.

Now, seeing once again the places where they had all lived together—back when life was young and contention had yet to divide their family—a wave of emotion must have washed over the old man.

While at Beersheba, Jacob offered sacrifices to God. That night, God spoke to Jacob in a vision: "I am God, the God of your father; do not be afraid to go down to Egypt, for I will make you a great nation there. I will go down with you to Egypt, and I will also surely bring you up again; and Joseph will close your eyes" (Gen.

46:3–4). By now, of course, Jacob knew of the brothers' betrayal of Joseph. God revealed to Jacob that the move to Egypt resulted from God's sovereign plan rather than from the sin of jealous sons. God took the initiative to bring about a major move in Jacob's life and in the lives of all those who would become the tribes of Israel.

I love the way God graciously encouraged Jacob to follow the Lord's leading. Allow me to paraphrase what God told Jacob: "I am God. Do not be afraid to go where I am leading you. My purposes for you are *there*, not here. I will go there with you."

By principle, these promises remain true for us as well. Like Jacob, we receive few specifics from God when he initiates change, but he gives everything we need to take the next steps. His Word, like a lamp, shows us only our next few steps. (Sometimes this means waiting.) And like Jacob, we have the assurance of God's presence with us—a promise Jesus also reiterated (see Matt. 28:20; John 14:16).

In leading us, God always goes with us.

As the journey neared its end, Judah rode ahead of the caravan to let Joseph know they approached Egypt. Joseph harnessed his chariot and raced to meet his father. Scripture describes the tender scene with simplicity: "As soon as he appeared before him, he fell on his neck and wept on his neck a long time. Then Israel said to Joseph, 'Now let me die, since I have seen your face, that you are still alive'" (Gen. 46:29–30).

Dream two: check. God's revelations to Joseph had come true.

What a beautiful reunion—one for which Joseph had waited on God for years and one his father had never even expected to see. Such is the grace of God, "who is able to do far more abundantly beyond all that we ask or think" (Eph. 3:20). Since it is more blessed to give than to receive, God must be most blessed of all—for no one has given more.

Sometimes we wait on God (without even knowing we're waiting) for blessings only he knows he'll give us.

9

WHEN FORGIVING SOMEONE
IS HARD

Now, therefore, it was not you who sent me here, but God.

Genesis 45:8

At some point today, pull out an old family photo album. You'll see snapshots of younger parents and yourself in numerous places. The memories will flow. Photographs capture more than moments of time. They save reminders. *I forgot about that blouse. Look how thin Dad used to be! Mom's handwriting seems the same.*

But the photos may summon painful memories as well. Many people who smiled alongside us in pictures years ago we find conspicuously absent today. As we do with the elephant in the room, we keep quiet about them. We rewrite our history because the prick of those names draws blood. But it's precisely *all* those memories—both the good and the bad—that give strength in times of struggle. Whenever I see pictures of years ago, and remember the pain associated with those moments, I also realize my family has persevered through those times. Somehow, with God's remarkable strength, we have endured.

Growing up in a godly home gives no guarantee you'll follow God. Likewise, a godless home doesn't doom you to a failed life. Sometimes the pendulum of godliness swings widely from generation to generation (see 2 Kings 21:1–2, 19; 22:1–2; 1 Chron. 3:13). The product of any home has more to do with a child's decisions than *simply* the parents' walks with God.

Was your home one in which the name of Jesus was honored? If so, emulate the lives of your parents but persistently pursue your own walk with Christ. Your parents' *godliness* isn't inherited. You are your own person before God. Your success in life comes by showing up faithfully, by making time with the Father the priority of your day, by embracing apologies and humility rather than thinking of them as threats to your ego, and by believing the best about your mate, your children, your siblings, your parents, and that friend of yours who offended you. These represent *your* decisions—and mine.

God wasn't asleep at the wheel the day he chose your family of origin. It came from the wisdom of his providential will, even though it may seem otherwise. You may have grown up in a godless, even abusive, family. Keep Joseph in mind as you filter your experiences through the truth of Scripture. Understand that God sovereignly allowed these things to occur—and not because of his carelessness or cruelty or indifference. Sovereignty often hides its reasons behind the veil of God's unimaginable insight.

As was the case with Christ's death on the cross—the most evil of all events that brought about the most good of all events—there remains a good purpose in your life from the evil you endured. I know that feels like a tough pill to choke down. Often we don't see the importance or significance of our early years until much,

much later. Sometimes only hindsight puts reason on the seeming cruelties of God's providence. Sometimes only heaven offers that hindsight. Either way, we're waiting on God.

Joseph would later tell his brothers, "You meant evil against me" (Gen. 50:20). Although he recognized the evil of their betrayal, he also saw himself as separate from their choices. Joseph made his own decisions, and his success stemmed from a commitment we also can adopt. It begins with correct thinking. The way our family treated us does not define us—even if we had a great home. Our upbringing is not *who* we are, although it certainly plays a part in *what* God uses to shape our lives. No other person's failure has to define our future.

Regardless of what age we figure this out, we need to see the generation of our lives as a line in the sand. Our family's past lies behind us, and our lives represent a point of no return—a line over which we will step and never step back.

One reason we love Joseph's story so much comes from the fact that we can identify with it right from the start. Especially if we came from a dysfunctional home, a broken home, or a home where we felt like the odd duck. Nobody has perfect parents, including our children. Nobody has perfect siblings, including our brothers and sisters.

Most of us read the story of Joseph and quickly identify with Joseph. After all, he's the main character. He's the underdog. He's the one who needs our support. He's the person who models the life we want to live in the face of trials. But honestly, we also identify with Joseph because we see his sorry lot in life as similar to our own. We're the sufferers in relationships. We're the targets of unfair treatment. We're the ones forgotten for years. We're the ones who have to forgive. *We're the victims.* We're Joseph.

Maybe all of that is reality, okay—*but it isn't all of reality*.

We also need to see ourselves in another part of the story—just as real, but tougher to admit. *We're the brothers*. We're impulsive. We're jealous. We treat family badly. We're control freaks. Our words cut like razors. *We make victims*. We're the brothers.

In reality, our coin has two sides. We live as Joseph, and we live as the brothers. We need to forgive. We need forgiveness.

Without a heart of cynicism and with a heavy dose of grace, we need to come to the place where we realize everybody in our lives will fail us to some degree. Everybody. Our parents will fail us. Our children will fail us. Our spouse, our boss, our friends, and even our pastor—all will fail us. And let me quickly add, we will also fail them.

But you know the most humbling reality?

We fail ourselves.

I know, I know, that sounds like Ebenezer Scrooge reciting the book of Ecclesiastes. But it's true. The prophet Jeremiah wrote of the barrenness we experience in life when we look to people for strength and security instead of to God (see Jer. 17:5–8). When we look to people as our foundation, our attitude becomes *Who will make me feel good today?* Oh, we never *say* that, but we seek it. Our life's quest can quickly become trying to find a person or situation—or anything—that will either make us feel good or make us feel nothing. Whether it's family or friends, those closest to us often fail our expectations the most because we expect the most from them. That kind of unhealthy dependence makes us slaves of our circumstances—a sure recipe for disaster.

Disappointment with people *can* make us cynical. But it can also have the opposite effect. It can sober us up to the reality that God never designed people as our goal. We must shed our idolatrous dependence on people and push back against our inclinations to put them in God's place, because, as Jeremiah wrote, "The heart is more deceitful than all else and is desperately sick; who can understand it?" (17:9).

We live as fallen individuals in an imperfect world, and no person or circumstance can possibly produce the exact ingredients for our stability, joy, and purpose. If we look to people to give us the joy only God can give, we will see ourselves as victims. People can never be our focus by way of meeting our needs—or they will fail us. Our satisfaction must come from elsewhere.

But if we realize that normal life *includes* experiences of hurt, rejection, and loss—just as the Son of God faced—we'll quit expecting the perfection now that only heaven will bring. Instead, we'll love people more and demand of them less.

Disappointment with people should draw us close to the One who will never, ultimately, disappoint. Being close to God frees us up to love people rather than need them.

When we think about it, Joseph easily could have sidestepped the whole reconciliation thing. He had the clout to do so. In fact, as soon as he rose to power and his brothers came and bowed down, he could have identified himself and dispatched an envoy to Canaan to save his father and his brothers' families. Or he could have remained anonymous behind his Egyptian disguise and provided for them all in secret. *Easily.* As far as I can tell, neither of these options would have violated God's dreams to Joseph.

When we have options like that, easy ones or hard ones, to which do we default?

The path of least resistance shows itself everywhere. It remains a fact of nature. A river always flows around a mountain rather than over it. Electricity will find the easiest route through a circuit. Labradors choose to sleep more than to run. Nature prefers the easier path—and human nature follows that pattern as well. We'll read a magazine rather than our Bibles, watch TV rather than play with our kids and grandkids, and lose our tempers rather than control them. Left alone, we'll make choices based on what gives us the least pain and the most pleasure. Following the path of least resistance can become a habit that guides our lives.

Instead of choosing between the easy option and the hard option, we should decide based on another yardstick: What's the *right* option? As strange as it sounds, we'll never find the life God wants for us by avoiding pain. It comes instead by choosing to do right, regardless of the pain.

Even pain has its place. Without the resistance of a barbell, a muscle stays flabby. Without the resistance of gravity, a car can't speed along the ground, or for that matter, stop. In the same way, only by facing the resistance in our lives can we grow and move forward.

When people run away from a problem, God sends them back to face it. A few runners in the Bible include Hagar, Jacob, Moses, Elijah, and Onesimus. Every one of them ran away from a hard situation and God sent them back. As contradictory as it sounds, they were running from the very will of God they were seeking.

One reason many people never see God working in their lives is because they never hang in there long enough for God to show his power. If we always quit when life gets hard, we live as if it's all up to us. We're the cause. Trapped in the corner we've painted ourselves in, we search for another place without pain—one we'll never find. It's a vicious cycle. When we always take the path of least resistance, we always find ourselves running. But God sends us back so that we can face the challenge, discover his sufficiency, and find the life he wants for us.

Joseph could have chosen an easier path: simple provision, anonymity, or even vengeance. He had the power to do any of these.

Instead, he chose the tougher path of reconciliation. But how?

Forgiveness is tough because the debt is real. Maybe your parents neglected or even abused you. Perhaps your spouse betrayed your wedding vows. Or maybe your best friend backstabbed you. Whatever your situation, someone hurt you so deeply you feel you may never recover. Their actions took something real from you, and it feels like, in order to forgive, you must surrender even more than they have already taken.

Sometimes, either willfully or unintentionally, we withhold forgiveness because it represents the one part of the situation we think we can control. Or we'll refuse to forgive as a kind of payback to our offender. But in truth, unforgiveness gives more misery to us than to anyone else. Significant depression results from this choice. With good reason, the Bible commands us, "Do not let the sun go down on your anger, and do not give the devil an opportunity" (Eph. 4:26–27). The wounds we have suffered at the hands of others hurt us deeply, but God can heal those wounds through forgiveness and time.

I'll write that again: *God can heal them*. He did with Joseph. He can with us.

Forgiveness begins, of all places, on our faces. Like Joseph's brothers, we all lie prostrate before One who has every right to condemn us.

Unwitting theologians of the 1970s wrote what could represent the anthem of every person. I'm referring to Steppenwolf's song "Born to Be Wild." Have you noticed you never had to teach your kids to sin? They brought the knack with them from the womb. In a world that makes bestsellers out of books like *I'm OK, You're OK*, truth comes as a tough sell. After all, who would buy a book called *I'm Totally Depraved, You're Totally Depraved*?

Amazingly, the bestselling book of all time begins with that very theme.

God created humanity in his image, but sin has marred that image. Corruption has extended to every part of our nature. Let's not blame-shift the doctrine of depravity to Calvinism. We see it clearly enough in the words of Paul (who quoted David): "There is none righteous, not even one; there is none who understands, there is none who seeks for God" (Rom. 3:10–11). As sinners, we have nothing in and of ourselves that can commend us to—or earn our favor before—a holy God.

Sin comes as part of our fallen nature. Kids prove this. So do you and I. We were born to be wild, and we never outgrow it.

(By the way, total depravity serves as a great apologetic that the Bible is true. After all, who would invent a religion that said you had no chance to get to heaven apart from the unmerited favor of a holy and just God? All other religions try to earn their way to God. Christianity alone confesses the impossibility of the idea.)

When God drags his rake across the surface of our hearts and up pops a beer can, we need to view the revelation as a blessing. Is it disappointing? Absolutely! It can feel downright devastating. But like a doctor who discovers a spot on a lung or a lump in a breast, we know it's better to acknowledge the problem and deal with it than to waste, and eventually lose, our lives because of our ignorance or disregard of the disease. However, knowing about it only makes it better *if* we deal with it.

The book of Proverbs has scores of verses about the person who refuses correction (see Prov. 12:15; 15:5; 17:10; 26:12). The fool takes no criticism because he thinks he has already arrived—and in a sad way, he has. He'll go no further because his ego allows no progress. With the fool, the problem always lies somewhere else. Anywhere but in the mirror. But shifting blame is neither beneficial nor honest. It takes no courage to point fingers. It takes tremendous guts to dig the lint out of your navel and examine it—and own it.

For some reason, when we feel convicted of sin our index finger sticks out. Finger pointing is hardwired into our hearts. In fact, it started early in human history. *Really* early. In the Garden of Eden, God confronted Adam and Eve after they sinned, and their reaction set the course for an entire race of blame-shifters. Adam shifted the blame to Eve (and to God), and Eve shifted the blame to the serpent (see Gen. 3:12–13). In spite of the devil's temptation and others' influences, God held Adam and Eve responsible for their own sins. They felt shame—which involves a deeper feeling of worthlessness as a person rather than guilt over an act of sin— and they snatched fig leaves to cover themselves. But forgiveness required the Lord to provide a sacrificial death on their behalf, atoning for their sin and covering their shame (see v. 21).

In the same way, God's plan for removing our guilt and shame involves removing the sin that caused it. Nothing has changed except the means of removal. Fig leaves in any form fail to cover our exposure. Only against the black backdrop of this bad news can we best appreciate the gospel, the "good news" of the grace of God. God sent his Son, Jesus, to die on a cross to pay the penalty we deserved for our sins, and Jesus rose again to prove he had paid in full. Anyone who believes receives forgiveness. It's that simple (see John 3:16; Rom. 4:25). In other words, when we recognize our sin and receive God's provision through the finished work of Christ on the cross, we have the forgiveness we craved when we shifted blame to somebody else.

With no sin, there's no need to feel shame—and no need to blame others.

Joseph's words to his brothers as they departed, "Do not quarrel on the journey" (Gen. 45:24), contained a kernel of grace that should sprout and spread.

Joseph urged them to extend grace to one another rather than blame-shift and accuse one another. The principle hidden in his words bursts forth with clarity in the New Testament: "Be kind to one another, tender-hearted, forgiving each other, just as God in Christ also has forgiven you" (Eph. 4:32). Notice the phrase "just as." Those words provide both our obligation and our motivation to forgive.

Forgiveness may begin on our faces before God, but it doesn't end there. The same grace we received, God commands we extend to others.

Jesus said it this way: "If you forgive others for their transgressions, your heavenly Father will also forgive you. But if you do not forgive others, then your Father will not forgive your transgressions" (Matt. 6:14–15). In short, if you as a Christian bear a grudge against someone, you are still saved, but you remain out of fellowship with God. Forgiving someone plays an essential role in your walk with the Lord.

Have you ever noticed the tenth commandment, "You shall not covet" (Exod. 20:17), is the only one of the Ten Commandments we obey or disobey in the heart? The first nine sins we can see, but only God sees number ten. One of the elders at our church, Dr. Stanley Toussaint, suggested that the tenth commandment might provide a hermeneutic—a means of interpretation—for the other nine. In other words, all the other commandments ultimately stem from the heart as well. That may be why, when Jesus gave his Sermon on the Mount, he pointed to anger, not murder, and to lust, not adultery, as the root problems for these sins (see Matt. 5:21–22, 27–28).

For forgiveness to count, we must forgive from the heart—and more than with our words.

But what if someone hurts us repeatedly? Will there ever come a point when we no longer have to forgive? Peter asked Jesus this very question (see Matt. 18:21–22). To what extent do we have to forgive? To paraphrase Jesus's concise answer: "To what extent have you been forgiven?" The Lord then added a motivation to our obligation: "Shouldn't you have had mercy on your fellow servant just as I had on you?" (v. 33 NIV).

Forgiveness and reconciliation *may* occur in the same moment, but often they happen years apart. Forgiveness begins in our hearts long before it gets expressed in reconciliation, and that truth carries other implications. Forgiveness means we refuse to hold a grudge, a promise we may have to remind ourselves of many times each day. But we also may need to establish boundaries for physical protection, because although forgiveness is given, trust is earned. An abused person should forgive his or her abuser, but forgiveness never requires such foolishness as putting oneself in harm's way again. Reconciliation may take a long time—after a person has earned trust.

Most of our situations lie outside of abuse or danger and deal primarily with attitudes. In these cases we need to evaluate the validity of the "boundaries" we prop up. They could simply be excuses to stay on the path of least resistance. Ideally, forgiveness should lead to reconciliation.

When Joseph reconciled with his brothers, clearly he had already forgiven them. He didn't wait for the grand finale to do so. Joseph had forgiven his brothers long before they showed up with hats in hand. Also, Joseph held back on reconciliation until God revealed they had changed.

We need to be careful in using this as an excuse. "They aren't ready," we may say, when in fact we mean we aren't willing. Waiting on God becomes an excuse when he has commanded us to forgive—and we refuse to.

When Judah gave his impassioned plea to Joseph, Joseph had already forgiven his brothers. His forgiveness of them had nothing to do with Judah's self-sacrificing courage or their positive reaction to the tests.

How did Joseph respond positively in forgiveness when so many events in his life were negative—even evil?

When it comes to forgiveness, no other principle has helped me more than this one from the life of Joseph. I believe the same can be true for you.

After Joseph identified himself to his brothers, he said more than once, "God sent me before you" (see Gen. 45:5–9). Five times in as many verses, Joseph attributed this whole affair to God's doing. Joseph believed in a *sovereign* God. In fact, in the same sentence we read "You sold me" and "God sent me"—seeming contradictions only the sovereignty of God can weave together.

Whenever Joseph opened his mouth, "God" came out. Joseph's words revealed the thoughts of his heart. He had learned to look to the Lord for strength and purpose. Trials proved it so. Only by relying on God could he resist Potiphar's wife, care about his fellow prisoners, and wait until the right moment to reconcile when his heart yearned to reconnect. Only with God as his foundation could he look beyond the evil deeds done to him and see a higher purpose for it all. Only an unfailing God could provide an immovable anchor.

The twenty-two-year-old echo, "Let us see what will become of his dreams!" (Gen. 37:20) is spun on its head in submission to a sovereign God. Ironically, the brothers' incredulous use of the Hebrew term for Joseph *ruling* over them in his dreams found its repetition from their lips as they tell their father Joseph is *ruler* of Egypt (see 37:8; 45:26). Joseph had become what his dreams revealed. The brothers sold Joseph to Egypt to get rid of him, but God sent Joseph to Egypt to deliver the brothers. More than merely a cruel act of humanity, Joseph's trip came about through the sovereign will of God.

Of course, God could have provided a different way to deliver Joseph's family from the famine. How about stopping the famine with a good downpour of rain? Or even better, preventing the famine in the first place! That would have saved lives. But it wouldn't have changed lives—and that was God's goal. God brings famines to change hearts—to make us into the individuals he wants us to be.

Loss in life can become one of God's greatest ways to cultivate grateful hearts. It comes from one simple word: *perspective*. And that type of perspective can occur at any moment. The car accident you survived makes you grateful for your family who irritated you the same morning. After an unexpected job loss, you feel thankful for the new position you have. The doctor's report of cancer in remission causes you to view each new day as the blessing it was to begin with.

Perspective makes all the difference.

I don't know about you, but as a teenager, I (thought I) knew just about everything. You could even say I felt omniscient. I marveled at the incompetence of grown-ups on the simplest of issues. They just didn't get it. And then I grew up and something strange happened. I discovered as an omniscient person I still had a lot to learn.

So many times I stood so sure of myself only to later discover my abject ignorance. For example, I knew a lot about God until I began to seriously study his Word. As it turned out, the more I learned about God the less I knew. The same proved true with marriage and family. Getting married enrolled me in a course of art, not science, and parenting has offered me a long study on my own selfishness. I've learned a lot since I became omniscient. But you know where that all-knowing teenager resurfaces the most in my life? Probably the same place it shows up in your life.

When we talk to God.

We think nobody better understands our needs than we do, so we take our omniscience straight to the Lord. We tell him how much better life would be if he would just (insert an omniscient request here). We even have verses to back up our ideas.

As it turns out, the Lord has plans for our plans, and they stem from his infinite wisdom. Paul expressed it well: "Oh, the depth of the riches both of the wisdom and knowledge of God! How unsearchable are His judgments and unfathomable His ways! For who has known the mind of the Lord, or who became His counselor?" (Rom. 11:33–34).

Consider a few of the major events in your life that you can trace to a chance conversation, a simple invitation, or a random bit of advice. Consider how you and your spouse or a good friend met for the first time. What were the chances of that connection occurring when you came from such different backgrounds? Think about a major job change you've had or a relocation of some kind. Chances are, although you made *some* decisions, the events unfolded in ways you never could have imagined or planned.

God has plans for our plans because his ways are unfathomable and unsearchable. We have, at best, only a superficial understanding of God's ways in our lives. He himself has told us, "As the heavens are higher than the earth, so are My ways higher than your ways and My thoughts than your thoughts" (Isa. 55:9).

If you can right now, take a look out a window at the sky. See any clouds or stars up there? Our all-wise, all-knowing, omniscient, and sovereign God has a mind *that* much higher than ours. The Lord needs no "counselor." Only he truly knows what will produce the best results in our lives. Plus, he thinks long-term, while we tend to plan only as far as the weekend.

God's plans to send Joseph to Egypt occurred long before he went there. Even though Joseph turned things around for the small Hebrew clan, Egypt would not always smile with favor on God's chosen people. There would arise a pharaoh who would forget Joseph. But even that played into God's plan. A century before Joseph, the Lord told Abram his descendants would endure oppression in a foreign land (see Gen. 15:13–16). Then after a delay of centuries, they would return to Canaan. The delay would come for what may have seemed like an odd reason: "the sin of the Amorites" (v. 16 NIV). God waited for the Amorites to respond before returning his people to the Promised Land—to go to war against them. That is sovereign grace.

You see, God sees the whole picture. He sees the traffic lights of the next century while we stare only at the red light in front of us. And although we may never comprehend God's sovereignty, we *can* believe in it. We can't understand all God knows, but we can understand that *he* understands it all.

That's called faith.

Joseph could forgive his brothers because he recognized he stood in the shadow of a sovereign God. Joseph chose to see every event in life through the filter of God's sovereignty, and so he knew he had the freedom to forgive. Joseph models the marvelous lesson that we can forgive others by factoring God's sovereignty into every event.

In faith, you can apply that truth to where you live today.

Bigger things are going on than the dead-end street of your victimization or problems.

God is at work.

Without a firm belief in a sovereign God, we see ourselves as the primary cause of life's events. We can even shrink to view God as distant, uninvolved, and irrelevant. Sovereignty paves a pathway of perspective that leads away from cynicism and bitterness to enthusiasm and grace.

The apostle Paul's faith in his sovereign Lord led him to view the hardships of God's servants with a victorious twist:

> We are afflicted in every way, but not crushed; perplexed, but not despairing . . . regarded as deceivers and yet true; as unknown yet well-known, as dying yet behold, we live; as punished yet not put to death, as sorrowful yet always rejoicing, as poor yet making many rich, as having nothing yet possessing all things. (2 Cor. 4:8; 6:8–10)

Scripture reminds us of a marvelous promise: "We know that God causes all things to work together for good to those who love God, to those who are called according to His purpose" (Rom. 8:28). This familiar verse sounds like an irrelevant cliché in permanent situations of pain—like death, divorce, mental handicaps, physical constraints, and so forth. This promise of God sounds thin when we interpret God working "all things . . . for good" as meaning good feelings or personal fulfillment or reasons we'll see in this lifetime that justify the pain we suffer.

But the promise in this verse has a context. The verses that follow Romans 8:28 speak of God working all things to make us like his beloved Son. *That* is the "good" God intends, and it takes a lifetime—and ultimately, it takes resurrection. So challenging are the "all things" we endure in life that these verses even affirm that in spite of all we endure, which seems to contradict God's goodness, nothing can separate us from God's love (vv. 29–39).

So although we may struggle and suffer at the hands of those who couldn't care less about us, nothing can prevent us from experiencing the plans of our sovereign God. The Lord will even use those who oppose us as part of the process—just like he did with Joseph's brothers. I like the perspective Dustin Shramek offers:

> Too often we allow ourselves to believe that a robust view of God's sovereignty in all things means that when suffering comes it won't hurt. God's sovereignty doesn't take away the pain and evil that confront us in our lives; it works them for our good.[1]

Joseph took the first step to forgive when he had the power to get even. He had the opportunity to stay anonymous, but he chose to reconcile.

Most likely, we have that same opportunity.

Often we hesitate to attempt reconciliation because we fear it may go south and make things worse. But what we fear seldom happens. Our worries rarely prove prophetic. Jacob feared his reunion with Esau, and Joseph's brothers feared Joseph. But both sets of worries proved needless, because God had worked below the surface to prepare both sets of hearts for reconciliation.

Like Joseph, we stand in the shadow of a sovereign God. In that place of security, we have commands to follow. The Lord Jesus required we reconcile with someone before we come to worship (see Matt. 5:23–25). The principle of reconciling with another before approaching God had its beginnings long before Jesus commanded it. One could even argue God confronted Cain with the principle by means of a simple question (see Gen. 4:9).

How do we begin the process of reconciliation? We start by showing love, and we quit waiting on the right moment or on the other person to make the first move. We push past the awkwardness and step off the path of least resistance. "Love your enemies," Jesus instructed, "do good to those who hate you, bless those who curse you, pray for those who mistreat you. . . . If you love those who love you, what credit is that to you? For even sinners love those who love them" (Luke 6:27–28, 32). An "enemy" doesn't mean, for us, a terrorist or some foreign invader. It means, for starters, that person who offends you. That other Christian who doesn't act like a Christian. That relative with a big mouth. That neighbor who weed-whacks your begonias. That jerk at work who takes the credit for your ideas. Often, instead, we deal with our neighbors by avoiding them. We pigeonhole them as irreconcilable and stay behind our sacrosanct boundaries. The path of least resistance has many trails—all downward.

The apostle Peter's words sound odd at first, but a second glance shows them to be helpful: "Since you have in obedience to the truth purified your souls for a sincere love of the brethren, fervently love one another from the heart" (1 Pet. 1:22). Why would he tell those who have a "sincere love" to "love one another"? Because Peter uses two different terms for *love* in the same verse.

The first, "sincere love," speaks of a friendly affection based entirely on feeling pleasure from someone's presence. This love offers no resistance and gives legitimate happiness. But because it has within it only feelings of pleasure, it can quickly evaporate. A love based on feelings never lasts because feelings always change. Honestly, most relationships never grow past this type of love.

The second love Peter referred to comes not from our feelings about someone but from that person's genuine value. When we choose to recognize the worth of another person, made in the image of God, we can add to our feelings a fervent love "from the heart." The first kind of love begins and ends with our emotions; the second begins and ends with our will. The second love gives strength to the first. One receives, and the other gives even when it gets nothing in return.

God describes this sacrificial love as patient, kind, not jealous, not arrogant, not selfish, and not provoked. This love bears all things, believes all things, hopes all things, and endures all things. It never fails (see 1 Cor. 13:4–8).

Just as we forgive others as God forgave us, so "we love, because He first loved us" (1 John 4:19). God commands we go beyond feeling love for one another to *showing* love for one another.

How do we show love when we don't feel like it? We reach out with the goal of love without expecting any love in return. We mail a birthday card or send a text with the simple words, "Thinking of you on this special day." We give a hug and don't react against their cold reluctance. For husbands and wives, Peter also gives inspired counsel that love expresses itself daily by maintaining respectful, godly behavior and a gentle and quiet spirit, and living in an understanding way (see 1 Pet. 3:1–9). Tough assignments, sure. But for Christians, they're nonnegotiable.

The motivation behind these acts of love? It must find its roots in our love for God. We cannot love others in order to receive love; that type of barter will always feel off balance in our favor. God has already loved us more than we could possibly imagine or repay.

Our love has no expectation or goal except the glory of God, and therefore we show our love for God by loving others. Love remains our only outstanding debt (see Rom. 13:8).

Sometimes when facing these tough conversations, all we see is the mountain before us, not the entire pathway God provides over it. But it's there. We should take the first step anyway. "Is the LORD's power limited?" the Lord asked Moses. "Now you shall see whether My word will come true for you or not" (Num. 11:23). We can still believe God without seeing or understanding his plan.

Some years ago I found myself at odds with another person after a conversation went south. This individual spoke severely to our daughter, and I confronted this person with the truth—but in anger, and I failed to speak the truth in love. Later, I tried to get together with this person to talk it through. I knew I needed to ask for forgiveness for how I had spoken. But others asked me to leave it alone for the time being. Although I tried to comply at first, I felt miserable keeping quiet. I came to realize I needed to ask forgiveness, no matter what. The only way I felt I could honor both the Lord and those in authority came by writing a letter and asking for forgiveness. I never heard back from the individual, nor did I expect to or need to. But I needed to do my part. I needed to reach out.

I really believe even when we know someone will refuse to forgive us, we need to ask anyway. *Genuinely.* We need to make it sincere and honest, done with such integrity that we can walk away knowing we have honored God. Paul qualified his command appropriately: "If possible, *so far as it depends on you*, be at peace with all men" (Rom. 12:18, emphasis added). They may reject us. They may say nothing. They may offer a glib, obligatory, "I'll try." But we have to gauge the success of our efforts by our obedience to God and not by other people's disobedience to him. That's between them and him. "Be patient with everyone," Paul urged (1 Thess. 5:14).

We cannot force what God has yet to change in another person. Sometimes God takes his time. After all, he has taken a long time with us, hasn't he?

Let's face it; other people in our lives may *never* choose to change. But neither do they have to change us. We can choose to follow God regardless, to forgive from the heart, and to move forward in genuine joy. God's sovereignty allows us all of that. Jesus died to give us that freedom.

Like Joseph, we can choose to respond in grace. We can completely release from bitterness and obligation all who have hurt us. I like how Mary DeMuth expresses it: "Everything that hurts us on earth has the potential, when we let God put His hands in the conflict, to bless the world. In short, we hurt, and God heals, which makes us an agent of healing."[2]

That was Joseph. He lived in light of God's sovereignty.

What makes Joseph's story such a good one is the reconciliation we enjoy seeing between him and his family. But we must remember—we *must* remember—these chapters of joyful reconciliation and resolution came at the end of a *huge* gap of twenty-two years in which Joseph waited on God. The Lord took a long, long time to bring resolution to relationships that hurt Joseph deeply.

In the midst of those years, God refined Joseph with trials, Judah had his own set of problems, and the other brothers also experienced God's sovereign hand of correction—culminating with a famine that threatened their financial security and their very lives. Sometimes it takes a lot to provoke change.

And of course, it takes time.

Waiting on God for someone else to change makes for long days. But we need to consider the Lord may have more in mind than a teary hug or firm handshake. In the long gap before the resolution, we really cannot presume God's only work will show itself in the *other* person's heart and attitude. After all, God refined Joseph too.

The Lord may actually have something for *us* to learn in the interim. While we wait on God to change someone else, God may be waiting on us to love that person.

When we look at Joseph weeping, trying to control himself, and rushing off to conceal his emotions, we see a man dealing with the struggle of waiting on God. He *wanted* to reconcile. He longed for the reunion with his brothers and his father, but he also knew to wait on God's timing. Even after he had the power to act on his own, Joseph waited.

You may have someone in your life with whom you're waiting for a long resolution. You may want resolution or reconciliation so badly you feel tempted to push it before God gives the green light. Keep your strong desire for relief obedient to the will of God so you don't undermine the very reconciliation you seek. Just as God often allows huge gaps of grace in our lives—that space where he gives *us* time to repent—so we need to extend those same gaps to others and give God room to work. He will make it clear when he wants you to take the next step beyond simple acts of love. God's green light will never contradict the Bible. Never.

In the meantime, as you wait on God, don't *ever* give up.

When my mother died unexpectedly, I really could have chosen to grow bitter against God, against her original divorce, against alcohol, or against a thousand other things—including myself. But somehow God's sovereignty poured grace in the cracks of my heart and reminded me that even graves are not the end of the story. Not even close.

Although we cannot fully understand God's sovereignty, we *can* fully believe in it. More than a mere doctrine, sovereignty offers magnificent comfort when everything we see seems to contradict everything God has promised. Without a firm faith in God's control of all things, we become anxious people who assume the direction of our lives is up to us. On the contrary, God has the plan in motion.

We walk a journey of discovery, and its end is glorious. For some of us, the resolutions we yearn for will come only at the very end—in glory.

Ultimately, that's what we're waiting on God for.

Part III

COMING HOME

10

The Hope of Dying with Unfulfilled Dreams

For Your salvation I wait, O Lord.

Genesis 49:18

The cold November wind seemed warm compared to the chill that ran up my spine. A group of us stood before an open grave as the minister began to speak.

"We have gathered here today to remember the life of Wayne Stiles," he said.

His words jarred me. I felt like I should check my watch to make sure the second hand was still moving. I had never heard those words before—much less in a cemetery.

My grandfather and I shared the same name, a fact I had always loved. So I felt honored when our family asked if I would pray at his graveside service. Regrettably, the minister had said nothing about Jesus, so I slipped the gospel into my prayer. I couldn't think of a better way to thank God for my grandfather's life and faith. Plus, I couldn't imagine what comfort anyone could hope to find at a memorial service that fails to point to the promises of God beyond the grave. Of course, we can honor a life well lived in the Lord—and we should—but the best way to honor our loved ones comes from speaking words they would want us to say. In addition to remembering their good life, we should point out that their eternal life has nothing to do with the good life they lived. God saved them by his grace. The message of salvation is what concerns the dead about the living. Even those who have died apart from God have this as their concern (Luke 16:27–31).

When we visit the cemetery of a loved one, we have nothing to see of the person except what we find chiseled on their tombstone. I'm convinced those engravings represent the most concise summaries on the planet. A person's entire life is summed up by the dash between the dates of their birth and death. A whole life—in a dash.

But the name, more than anything else, remains the most precious part of the gravestone. When we look at the stone, we look most often at the name. A name represents *a person*—including every part of their personality, every memory we have of them, and every conversation we shared with them.

Sometimes when I'm on my way through Sanger, Texas, I'll stop by its cemetery and visit my mother's grave. As I did that recently, I ran my fingers over the etching of her name. I lingered over her memory and thought about experiences we'd had together. After ten years without her, the closest I could come to embracing my mom was to touch the engraving of her name.

Joseph no doubt experienced similar feelings after his father dispatched him so many years earlier to check on the welfare of his brothers. On his fateful journey toward Shechem, Joseph would have stopped at his mother's tomb and remembered the grief he felt as a little boy when his mother died giving birth to his brother Benjamin. Rachel's tomb remained a known location for centuries, last mentioned in the days of King Saul—hundreds of years after Rachel died (see 1 Sam. 10:2). Even today, Israel has a kibbutz near Bethlehem called Ramat Rachel (but this traditional site of the matriarch's tomb mismatches with biblical geography).

Nostalgia over his mother's death would have washed over Joseph again many years later, as his father now lay on his deathbed in Egypt.

Joseph's father and brothers had lived in Egypt for seventeen years. Joseph had cared for them by asking of Pharaoh that he allow them to live in the best of the land—in Goshen. There these sons of Jacob made their homes and raised their families and lived under the protection and provision of Joseph. Genesis omits the details of these years as another long gap in a narrative punctuated only with key events. Jacob's death, after 147 years of life, offers one of the most significant of these occasions.

Nothing puts life in better perspective than death. Death boils life down to its essentials, and the deathbed has witnessed many words that those left behind should have heard more often. Jacob's final words are a classic example.

As Jacob approached death, Joseph came to his father, who made an unusual request:

> "Place now your hand under my thigh and deal with me in kindness and faithfulness. Please do not bury me in Egypt, but when I lie down with my fathers, you shall carry me out of Egypt and bury me in their burial place." And [Joseph] said, "I will do as you have said." He said, "Swear to me." So he swore to him. Then Israel bowed in worship at the head of the bed. (Gen. 47:29–31)

Placing one's hand "under the thigh" of another meant placing a hand beneath the sexual organ (compare 24:2). "Take my life in your hands," might be a way to paraphrase the euphemism that introduced Jacob's solemn request of Joseph. The land God promised to Abraham's descendants remained a key issue of faith for those who came after him. Jacob requested Joseph bury him in Canaan, in the same place Abraham and Isaac lay. Such a burial demonstrated faith in God's promises.

Joseph later brought his two sons to see his father on his death-bed, and "Israel collected his strength and sat up in the bed" (48:2). As the old man spoke, the matters closest to his heart spilled out first. Even after all this time, Jacob grieved the loss of Joseph's mother, Rachel, speaking of the grave he dug and also of its location. Jacob told how God Almighty reiterated to him at Bethel the promise given to Abraham and Isaac, the unconditional covenant that included the Promised Land, many descendants, and world-wide blessing (see 12:1–3; 28:14). Jacob told Joseph that his two sons, Ephraim and Manasseh, would inherit portions of the land of Canaan on the level of Jacob's other sons. That's why we have no tribe of Joseph. Jacob gave Joseph the double portion due the firstborn, and so Ephraim and Manasseh became tribes in their own right (see 1 Chron. 5:1–2).

As Joseph's two sons approached their grandfather, he kissed the boys, embraced them, and turned to Joseph with a tender insight: "I never expected to see your face, and behold, God has let me see your children as well" (Gen. 48:11). Compare this splendid reflection on God's grace to the statement Jacob made years earlier in a moment of despair: "Joseph is no more, and Simeon is no more, and you would take Benjamin; all these things are against me" (42:36). Remember those words? The circumstances served as one of the most extreme moments of tension and testing in Jacob's life. He thought he had lost two sons and would soon lose another.

Instead, God would give him Joseph back as well as Joseph's two sons.

Only God can perform such reversals.

There's not much we can be sure of today. We live in a culture of broken promises, broken relationships, shallow friendships, and flawed leaders. And that's just at church.

After a number of stabbing disappointments, we can come to the place where we expect little else. We can choose to hope for nothing in hopes we won't be disappointed. When we focus on the here and now—and especially on all the pain life has handed us—the black hole of hopelessness sucks us in and surrounds us.

When we consider the marvelous promise that "God causes all things to work together for good to those who love God, to those who are called according to His purpose," we also need to ponder the rhetorical question that follows: "If God is for us, who is against us?" (Rom. 8:28, 31). The question gives context to those painful parts of God's sovereignty in our lives. Of course, we *will* have many who oppose us. But godly hope comes as we realize that those who stand against us don't matter when God is for us, because nobody can stand against God.

In moments of great pain, theology offers us a strong anchor of the soul: *truth* we cling to in a sea of swirling emotions. In spite of all we endure in times of grief, pain, and confusion, nothing we experience *or feel* can separate us from Christ's love (see Rom. 8:38–39). In a world that fails us and disappoints us, we need to cling to the One who never will.

God offers true hope—a certain future with a specific outcome. This hope wildly contrasts with the rickety hope the world props up. Only God can make good on his promises.

"All these things are against me," Jacob said. And yet, just the opposite proved true! All those things—without exception—played a part in bringing about tremendous blessing for Jacob. Such is the grace of God.

God is for us. So who can stand against us?

The contrast of Jacob's perspectives here urges us to stop assigning hopelessness to the agony we feel in any given moment or circumstance. The sharpness of our pain deceives us as to its permanence, yet how often have we seen God turn pain on its head and provide blessings instead? We only need to wait on God. Pain and patience often walk in tandem. In fact, the word *patience* comes from a Latin term that means "suffering." That's why the old-fashioned adjective "long-suffering" serves as a synonym for patience. They go together.

Think about Jacob's words to Joseph: "I never expected to see you again, and now God has let me see your sons." Maybe God requires us to wait on him in our struggles so that his solution can prove bigger than our expectations could ever imagine. He may choose to provide blessings that correspond with his ability rather than with our understanding.

We may think we know the most generous and spectacular solution God could provide for us—usually an immediate one. But he knows the resolution that will astound and bless not only us but others also.

Old age had deprived Jacob of clear eyesight, as had also happened with his father, Isaac, on his deathbed (see Gen. 27:1). So when Joseph brought his sons before the 147-year-old patriarch for blessing, Joseph positioned his firstborn, Manasseh, so that he would correspond with Jacob's right hand—the place of preeminence.

But instead, the old man crossed his arms and placed his right hand on Ephraim's head—on the younger son.

"Not so, my father," Joseph objected, and gripped his father's hand to remove it, "for this one is the firstborn. Place your right hand on his head" (48:18). Joseph supposed his father's poor eyesight had caused him to mistake one son for the other. But in spite of his eyesight, Jacob saw more than Joseph did in this case.

Jacob crossing his arms had more to do with vision than it did with seeing.

A life of hard-learned wisdom lay behind Jacob's tender response: "I know, my son, I know. . . . However, his younger brother shall be greater than he" (v. 19). We can almost see Jacob nodding his head in patient understanding. He had duped his blind father, Isaac, into blessing him, the younger son. The painful journey Jacob had lived after that taught him that God often acts contrary to what we expect. Finally, Jacob crossed his arms and surrendered to God's unusual leading.

Of all people, Joseph should have known, or perhaps should have anticipated, that God may rank his younger son higher than his firstborn. After all, Abraham chose Ishmael, but God chose Isaac. Isaac chose Esau, but God chose Jacob. Jacob chose Joseph and then Benjamin, the "son of my right hand," but God would choose Judah. Joseph chose Manasseh, but God chose Ephraim. Even when Judah's sons were born of Tamar, the "younger" twin shoved his way out first (see Gen. 38:27–30).

We can go figure all we want, but we never will figure out God's plan.

God often crosses his arms. He regularly does the exact opposite of what we expect or want. We bring our desires, time after time, to God's right hand. But he gives them his left. We long to find success in one part of life, but God blesses another area we never anticipated. We bring a lifetime of planning, best practices, dreams, and goals to the Lord, and he redirects us on another path altogether.

"No, Lord, bless *this*, not that!" we protest, as if God needs glasses.

Over time we come to hear his tender voice: "I know, my son, I know. I understand, my daughter, I really do. But my thoughts are not your thoughts. My judgments are unsearchable and my ways unfathomable. I'm choosing to do it my way, a better way—a way you'll come to understand as better one day. But for now, you

need to trust me" (see Isa. 55:8–9; Rom. 11:33). Jennifer Rothschild puts it this way: "We will experience greater peace when we
love and trust a God we may not understand rather than when
we constantly try to conform him into an image we have created
in our imagination."[1]

I love how the Spirit of God surveyed Jacob's 147 years and
selected this occasion as the crowning event of his faith. The New
Testament records it in brief terms: "By faith Jacob, as he was
dying, blessed each of the sons of Joseph, and worshiped, leaning
on the top of his staff" (Heb. 11:21). Jacob had such confidence
in God's will that he crossed his arms and blessed Joseph's sons
accordingly—believing they would one day inherit portions of
the Promised Land. This event most characterized Jacob's faith
because it revealed promises Jacob would never see fulfilled in his
lifetime. His faith enabled him to see beyond tradition and even
beyond the grave.

After blessing Joseph's boys, Jacob assembled all his sons, "the
twelve tribes of Israel," to pronounce blessings on each of them,
"every one with the blessing appropriate to him" (Gen. 49:28).
So, for some sons, like Reuben, the blessing "appropriate to him"
came as an official forfeiture of what he could have had.

As Jacob's firstborn son, Reuben had the privilege of preeminence among his brothers. That meant after Jacob died, Reuben
would have become the leader. However, as we've mentioned
before, Reuben tried to seize the right of the firstborn prematurely by having relations with Bilhah, his father's concubine.
Reuben's presumption backfired. In trying to take too soon a
position that would be his, Reuben lost it altogether (see Gen.
35:22; 49:3–4).

I also find it interesting that centuries later Reuben's tribe, instead of entering the Promised Land under Joshua, chose to settle
on the eastern side of the Jordan River. To them, the land around
the Medaba Plateau, overlooking the Dead Sea, looked preferable

to the land God had promised. History records the unavoidable problems they faced as a result, having chosen to settle so close to the Moabites and Ammonites. Like their forefather before them, Reuben's descendants refused to wait for God's best and settled instead on second best.

In the same way, our privileges and abilities can tempt us to see them as a guarantee of success. But these opportunities can become handicaps when mingled with presumption. Consider the gifted artist with an arrogance that keeps him unemployed. Or the beautiful woman with an attitude that makes her unattractive. Or the young person brought up in a Christian home who abandons morality for the sake of curiosity or impatience. In each case, their privileges, gifts, or strengths became their weaknesses because they neglected to yoke them to simple, daily obedience.

The same proved true with Simeon and Levi. Jacob described them as "brothers," not because they had the same mother but because they acted in the same manner by violence and vengeance (49:5). They avenged the rape of their sister Dinah by massacring the men of Shechem. As a result of their fierce and cruel anger, Jacob said, "I will disperse them in Jacob, and scatter them in Israel" (v. 7). Interestingly, the priestly tribe of Levi would come to have no allotment in the Promised Land, but the tribe would find itself scattered across Israel in forty-eight levitical cities. Furthermore, Simeon's tribe had their portion of land ultimately swallowed up by Judah. Jacob's words proved true.

The tragedy of Reuben, Simeon, and Levi is what could have been. They never would have acted as they had if they knew the far-reaching consequences of their impulses. They show us, from their acts of insubordination, that we can disqualify ourselves from the very benefits our privileges intended to offer us.

Even though we cannot change the past that has happened, we can change the past that will be. Faithfulness today allows us to change the past, in a sense, because today is tomorrow's yesterday.

Living in light of that truth, we can change the past that will be by walking closely with God today.

As far back as the rivalry between Rachel and Leah—the mothers of Joseph and Judah, respectively—the narrative carries a suspense as to which tribe would have the birthright of Jacob and the blessing of Abraham's covenant.

No doubt, Joseph stands as the hero of the story. Some Bible students even go so far as to call him a "type" of Christ. After all, Joseph, like Jesus, came to his brothers with the promise from God that he would rule them, but they rejected him and gave him up for dead. But behold, he lives and rules the earth! The similarities seem striking, for sure. But I prefer a more exacting view of biblical types of Christ—namely, those types the Bible actually suggests as such—such as Adam, Melchizedek, and Isaac (see Rom. 5:14; Heb. 7:1–3; 11:18–19). Otherwise, we can make "types" of anyone or anything (I've heard some loo-loos). It's also tough to find a purpose for these subjective associations.

When Jacob pronounced Joseph's blessing in Genesis 49:22–26, the word *blessing* appears multiple times. Indeed, God blessed Joseph for his faithfulness. Not only that, if the first three sons lost the privilege because of their sin, then it makes sense that we could skip *all* the sons who sold Joseph into slavery and just plant the flag of blessing in the line of Ephraim—Joseph's blessed son.

If we were to guess, we would wager that the blessing God promised to Abraham would pass through Joseph.

But God crossed his arms.

Although Joseph's tribe of Ephraim would prove extremely significant in the centuries that followed, the blessing of Abraham, Isaac, and Jacob—the line of the Messiah—would flow to all nations through the fourth son of Jacob and Leah: *Judah*. Jacob's words are pregnant with meaning:

> Judah, your brothers shall praise you; your hand shall be on the neck of your enemies; your father's sons shall bow down to you. Judah is a lion's whelp; from the prey, my son, you have gone up. He couches, he lies down as a lion, and as a lion, who dares rouse him up? The scepter shall not depart from Judah, nor the ruler's staff from between his feet, until Shiloh comes, and to him shall be the obedience of the peoples. He ties his foal to the vine, and his donkey's colt to the choice vine; he washes his garments in wine, and his robes in the blood of grapes. His eyes are dull from wine, and his teeth white from milk. (vv. 8–12)

While Joseph's dreams revealed he would rule over his family, the dreams never suggested perpetual leadership. Jacob's blessing of Judah, however, was different. It included a prediction that *began* similar to Joseph's dreams—"Your father's sons shall bow down to you"—but then it went *beyond* it: "The scepter shall not depart from Judah" (v. 10). Although Joseph received the rights of the firstborn, Judah's tribe would have the permanent preeminence of kingly leadership, denoted by a scepter, the staff of a sovereign.

The leadership would remain with the tribe of Judah, Jacob said, "until Shiloh comes" (v. 10). When American historians hear the word *Shiloh*, they think of the Civil War battle that occurred near Pittsburg Landing in southwestern Tennessee. Baby Boomers who hear the word may start humming the chorus to a Neil Diamond song. But a variant of the Hebrew word *shiloh* literally means "whose it is," and the NIV renders it well: "until he comes to whom it belongs." The "it" refers to the scepter Jacob promised to Judah's tribe. Ezekiel would later speak of removing the crown from Judah's worthless king "until He comes whose right it is, and I will give it to Him," a clear reference to Jacob's words to Judah (Ezek. 21:27). Interestingly, when the Hebrews settled in the Promised Land centuries later under Joshua, they named the site where the presence of God dwelt in the tabernacle Shiloh—an unwitting connection to Jesus, who "became flesh, and did tabernacle among us" (John 1:14 YLT).

So sure are most theologians that *Shiloh* has messianic overtones that they capitalize the word into a proper name: "until Shiloh comes." Rightly so, for Jesus came from the tribe of Judah, and the apostle John makes a direct tie to Jacob's prophecy by referring to our Lord as "the Lion that is from the tribe of Judah, the Root of David" (Rev. 5:5). Furthermore, the metaphors that Jacob included in Judah's prophecy involved an abundance of milk and wine—a time of prosperity Scripture reveals will occur during the Messiah's kingdom (see Isa. 65:21–25; Zech. 3:10). Significantly, Jesus's first miracle provided abundant wine, a sign that the kingdom he offered to Israel he could, in fact, deliver (see John 2:1–11). Even before his birth, the angel said of Jesus, "He will reign over the house of Jacob forever, and His kingdom will have no end" (Luke 1:33).

I doubt Jacob fully understood the weight of his final words that day.

We have referred only to the five most significant tribes of the twelve. Of these five, two stand taller than the rest: Judah and Ephraim, Joseph's dominant tribe. Joseph got Jacob's birthright, but Judah received Jacob's blessing—the leadership and the line of the Messiah (see 1 Chron. 5:1–2; Ps. 78:67–68). In the centuries that followed, these two tribes constantly locked horns over national control. In fact, so intense was the rivalry between them that when God settled them in the Promised Land, he placed the tribe of beloved Benjamin as a buffer between them (see Josh. 18:11).

When the nation of Israel divided after King Solomon's death, Ephraim took ten tribes to the north, and Judah and Benjamin remained alone in the south. Sadly, the tribes headed by Joseph's descendants apostatized against the Lord. Only Judah remained faithful. We get the New Testament designations "Jew" and "Judea" from the name Judah.

The man Judah, the first of his tribe to offer his life in exchange for his brother, would pass the scepter down through the centuries to Jesus, the One who laid down his life for us all.

Rather than read Genesis as a collection of independent stories, like chapters in a storybook, we need to understand the book as one story with many parts. The story of Joseph only serves the larger story of Judah, and Judah merely serves the larger story of the Messiah predicted to come who would crush the serpent's head—a theme that bookends all sixty-six books of the Bible (see Gen. 3:15; Rev. 12:9; 20:2).

Our lives follow the same divine principle. Rather than fixate on why God has allowed a particular painful chapter in our lives, we need to remember that God has the big picture in mind and each chapter plays a part of the whole. Focusing on just one part of our life story and our discouragement can consume us. If, instead, we focus on God's big picture, we find strength to push through, to hang on, to press forward instead of shrinking in despair.

Taking it a step farther, our solitary life represents only one of many billions that play a part in God's grand plan for the ages. We need to be content with playing a small but significant part in God's metanarrative of history.

That doesn't mean we're insignificant. It means God is far more significant than we ever imagined.

It's all about him.

In the middle of Jacob's words of blessing to his twelve sons, suddenly, he paused and did a strange thing. Wedged between the sidebar blessings to Dan and Gad, Jacob uttered these significant words: "For Your salvation I wait, O Lord" (Gen. 49:18).

Jacob prayed.

Only three words in the Hebrew text, Jacob's concise prayer reveals the first time the word *wait* has fallen from his lips. The verb appears in its intensive form and means more than merely waiting, but *eagerly waiting*. For that reason, the term also can mean "to hope." Although this isn't the first time Jacob has waited on God, it does reflect the first time he has chosen to do so—amazingly, here at the end of his life. And expressed in prayer.

Jacob said he waited for the Lord's "salvation." The word often refers to rescue from external troubles, but because of its context at the end of Jacob's life—appearing in the midst of his blessing the tribes of Israel—the word also carries significant prophetic overtones. Jacob knew that only God could bring about the fulfillment he promised. For this, Jacob eagerly waited. For this covenant, Jacob hoped. And although we cannot make too much of it in this context, the name of our Lord Jesus would come from the basic root of Jacob's word for salvation, *yeshua* (see Matt. 1:21).

After blessing his sons, Jacob repeated his request they bury him in Canaan rather than in Egypt. And having said this, the patriarch "drew his feet into the bed and breathed his last" (Gen. 49:33).

Then Jacob lay completely motionless.

Joseph threw himself on his father and wept over him, as his brothers also must have done. He then commanded the Egyptians to embalm his father, and, with Pharaoh's permission, they began the journey to carry Jacob's body back to Canaan for burial.

Instead of the direct route through Beersheba up to Hebron, the procession took a longer, circuitous course along the Dead Sea to the threshing floor of Atad, beyond the Jordan River (see Gen. 50:11). The location of the site is uncertain—as is the reason for the detour to it. But if it lay near Jericho, as some suggest, this entrance into Canaan would have foreshadowed the fulfillment of Jacob's belief that God would bring the tribes into the Promised Land one day, poignantly, by a similar circuitous route.

Furthermore, if Joseph and his brothers ascended the hill country via the route Joshua would later use, they would have carried Jacob's body past Luz (Bethel), where God had promised the land to Jacob in a dream, and also past Rachel's tomb—both sites that Jacob mentioned on his deathbed (see Gen. 48:3–4, 7).

Seventeen years had passed since Joseph's brothers had set foot in Canaan. But for Joseph himself, his memory had to stretch back almost forty years to a time when, as a seventeen-year-old young man, he left his father to check on his brothers. It had been a long, long time since he'd worn his coat of many colors.

Reminiscences must have flooded Joseph's mind and emotions as he beheld the places he had forgotten he knew. The shapes of the foothills, the winding of their paths, the color of the limestone beneath the trees. Every corner and crag held a memory. Some were of Benjamin as a baby. Others were of his brothers' hurtful words. But mostly, he would have thought of his father. After all, that's why they came back here. Joseph spent the first seventeen years of his life with his father in Paddan-Aram and Canaan—and the last seventeen years of his father's life with him in Egypt.

The last time Joseph had walked in Hebron, his father walked with him. He'd held Joseph's hand and embraced him. But now, his father was gone.

The place where someone chooses to get buried is always significant. But in Israel, a burial place often expressed one's faith.

The cave of Machpelah served as the burial ground for the Hebrew patriarchs and their wives (see Gen. 23:19; 25:9; 49:30; 50:13). When Jacob's grandfather Abraham purchased the plot and its cave in order to bury his wife Sarah, he demonstrated faith in the Lord's covenant to give him *all* the land one day. But when? It's pretty tough to inherit something after you're dead.

Abraham, Isaac, and Jacob and their many descendants would die before ever receiving all God swore to give them. "All these died in faith, without receiving the promises," the book of Hebrews reminds us, "having confessed that they were strangers and exiles on the earth" (Heb. 11:13).

Either God reneged on his promise to Abraham, or the promise proves—and even demands—a resurrection.

When Jacob requested burial in Canaan, he revealed his faith that in death God's people lose nothing of God's promises, because his promises extend beyond the grave to the next life.

After burying Jacob in the cave of Machpelah, the sons of Israel made their way back to their home away from home. As Joseph left Hebron for the last time in his life, I wonder if he turned around and stood backward in his chariot, remembered his father once again, and waved. Thirty-nine years earlier he had waved goodbye to his father.

Now he said goodbye for the last time. The next reunion would have no more goodbyes.

The loss of their father grieved the sons. But it also removed for Joseph's brothers their sense of security. They feared that without their father alive, the brakes would be off—and Joseph would now exact vengeance on them.

> So they sent a message to Joseph, saying, "Your father charged before he died, saying, 'Thus you shall say to Joseph, "Please forgive, I beg you, the transgression of your brothers and their sin, for they did you wrong."' And now, please forgive the transgression of the servants of the God of your father." (Gen. 50:16–17)

Understandably, Joseph broke down and wept again. How utterly disheartening to have forgiven someone, to have expressed tenderness and compassion, only to have your genuine intentions doubted so many years after the fact. All that time Joseph thought his brothers and he had completely reconciled—only to discover their guilty consciences had given them no permanent peace. Somehow that elephant had wandered back into camp. Fearing that Joseph only "forgave" them for the sake of their father, they attempted to bring their father with them in the form of a phony petition. They even brought God into the plea.

Joseph's response dripped with grace and echoed what he had told them originally: "Do not be afraid, for am I in God's place? As for you, you meant evil against me, but God meant it for good in order to bring about this present result, to preserve many people alive" (vv. 19–20).

His words remain one of the classic theological statements in the Bible on the sovereignty of God. Joseph continued to cling to the truth he had expressed to them seventeen years earlier (see 45:5). He factored God's sovereignty into forgiveness, recognizing that even though what they did was evil, God nevertheless meant it for good.

They saw the evil events only from a human perspective—and expected vengeance. Joseph urged them to look higher—and to receive forgiveness.

Joseph's words to his brothers are also God's gift to us. Much more than a platitude to hang on a wall plaque, the truth of his words offers us the courage we need to trust God in the face of the pain, and even the evil, we experience.

Any attempt to explain the struggles in our lives will likely feel insufficient. That's why knowing *why* something happened seldom helps. We need to know *who* more than why. Sovereignty sees every event through the lens of God's purpose, although his purpose may remain hidden from us. God's sovereignty gives us the freedom to forgive others.

Our response to those events all boils down to faith. Do we trust God or not? Is he in control or isn't he? In these painful seasons, the Lord comforts us more by his presence than by his explanations. Reason alone never seems to satisfy—or to justify—our pain. We need God himself.

The events of Joseph's life illustrate that our greatest difficulties give us our greatest opportunities to demonstrate our faith in a sovereign God (see Acts 2:23; 4:28; 13:27; Phil. 1:12). Although the Lord causes all things to work together for good in the lives of believers, we seldom, if ever, will understand *how* his good comes from the great pain we experience.

But that's okay. Faith believes God anyway. Faith trusts the Lord in spite of the bloody tunics we get handed. Faith trusts in God's sovereignty even when our dysfunctional families do their thing. Faith chooses to forgive and to reach out in love rather than to cling to our rights as victims. Faith knows that God's promises will never fail us, even though we find ourselves in a pit, or in temptation, or falsely accused, or in a prison, or in strained family relationships, or being misunderstood.

Or even facing death. God's promises never fail.

Because death boils life down to its essentials, our own death remains our last and greatest opportunity to show our faith in a sovereign God. Joseph demonstrated faith by honoring Jacob's wishes to rest in Canaan. Then Joseph made the same request himself when it came time for him to die.

Many years later, at the age of 110, Joseph told his brothers, "I am about to die, but God will surely take care of you and bring you up from this land to the land which He promised on oath to Abraham, to Isaac and to Jacob. . . . And you shall carry my bones up from here" (Gen. 50:24–25). Even though Joseph had lived in Egypt the last ninety-three years of his life, he chose his final resting place based on the future, not the past.

For this great man of God, the Bible records but a simple account of his death. The final verse of Genesis also offers the final verse of Joseph's life: "So Joseph died at the age of one hundred and ten years; and he was embalmed and placed in a coffin in Egypt" (Gen. 50:26).

When Jacob had come from Canaan to Egypt, Joseph had raced his chariot to greet his father. But now, I like to imagine, Joseph rode on angelic chariots of fire to paradise for an unspeakably joyful reunion with his father and with his God, whom Joseph had served so faithfully all his life (see 2 Kings 2:11; 6:17).

The pyramids of Egypt stand as history's massive and most enduring tombs. In fact, the Giza pyramid remains the only one of the seven wonders of the ancient world still standing. Reserved almost exclusively for royalty, the pyramids had already stood for centuries when Joseph ruled the land. And yet we will never unearth hieroglyphics that point to a pyramid for Zaphenath-paneah— Joseph's Egyptian name.

The Bible says Joseph's body rested in a "coffin"—or a sarcophagus. Why a sarcophagus? Portability. Joseph's body was likely temporarily interred in a mastaba—a rectangular tomb about eighteen feet high—in the city of Dahshur. Centuries later, during the exodus, the Israelites took his body with them (by destroying his mastaba, which has been excavated and found to be both destroyed and bodiless).[2]

After the conquest of Canaan under Joshua, the Hebrews "buried the bones of Joseph, which the sons of Israel brought up from Egypt, at Shechem, in the piece of ground which Jacob had bought . . . and they became the inheritance of Joseph's sons" (Josh. 24:32). They buried Joseph's bones in Shechem, the very place Jacob sent Joseph to go check on his brothers. When Jacob lay on his deathbed, he had told Joseph, "I give you one portion more than your brothers" (Gen. 48:22). It's more than a coincidence that the word *portion* in Hebrew is the same spelling as *Shechem*. Many centuries later, the apostle John recorded that Jesus came near Shechem, "near the parcel of ground that Jacob gave to his son Joseph" (John 4:5).

Joseph had a firm confidence in God to the end. In fact, when the Holy Spirit chose to record a defining event of the life of Joseph, the Lord bypassed Joseph's purity in resisting Potiphar's wife as well as his diligence in the prison and in the palace, and even his confidence in God's promises in spite of impossible circumstances. God looked beyond Joseph's faithfulness and chose instead to record his faith in the face of death: "By faith Joseph, when he was dying, made mention of the exodus of the sons of Israel, and gave orders concerning his bones" (Heb. 11:22).

Why so much concern about the place of burial? Because the Promised Land remained a central part of the covenant God had made with Abraham. Burial in that land—even before owning any of it—demonstrated faith that death has no effect on the promises of God. Death is not the end.

God can raise the dead.

The first time Joseph was raised up from the pit in that region, he was sold as a slave. The next time Joseph rises from the ground, it will be to enter the earthly kingdom of God.

The idea of resurrection showed up long before the first Easter Sunday. In fact, when God commanded Abraham to sacrifice his son Isaac—the son through whom God's promises would come—Abraham understood "that God is able to raise people even from the dead, from which he also received [Isaac] back as a type" (v. 19).

When believers die, how else but through resurrection can God keep his promises to them? No other way.

During the time of the exile in sixth-century BC, the prophet Ezekiel spoke for the Lord God to the Jews: "I will open your graves and cause you to come up out of your graves, My people; and I will bring you into the land of Israel. . . . I will put My Spirit within you and you will come to life" (Ezek. 37:12, 14). The prophet went on to illustrate that Judah and Joseph—the two dominant tribes that represented the divided nation before the exile—would one day come together in unity under the leadership of King David.

Ezekiel's vision of dry bones gives us a broad overview of a believing Jew's end-times expectation: to rise from the dead with God's Spirit, to dwell in the Promised Land, and to live forever under the leadership of the Messiah—"the Lion that is from the tribe of Judah, the Root of David" (Rev. 5:5).

In speaking of Jacob, Joseph, and many other Old Testament saints, the writer to the Hebrews said it this way:

> All these died in faith, without receiving the promises, but having seen them and having welcomed them from a distance, and having confessed that they were strangers and exiles on the earth. . . . But as it is, they desire a better country, that is, a heavenly one. Therefore God is not ashamed to be called their God; for He has prepared a city for them. (Heb. 11:13, 16)

Of course, these words apply to us as well. This chapter of Hebrews begins with what we often consider a definition of faith: "Now faith is the assurance of things hoped for, the conviction of things not seen" (v. 1). But it's more than a mere definition. The verse begins with the verb *is*, and its present tense means faith has a place of continual application in our lives.

We live with the continual hope of promises we don't yet see.

Like Joseph and the Hebrews of old, we have an eager expectation for the time when we shall have no more tears or crying or pain. That's a promise. But as of yet, it hasn't happened. The Word of God has many such promises. The Hebrews all died without receiving the promises, and yet *they saw them from a distance*.

We need to learn to see life that way too.

And we can.

11

WHAT YOU'VE
BEEN WAITING FOR

*God will surely take care of you, and you shall carry my
bones up from here.*

Genesis 50:25

What can we do when the life God has given us seems so
different from the life he has promised us? Different
people handle that tension in different ways.

Most people live for dreams. It's a quest, really. Clinging to ide-
als of how life could be and should be, they chase those dreams
like a carrot dangling from a stick. Always within reach, it seems,
but never gotten.

I guess we're all wired to pursue the ideal. The world calls it
"following your heart," and we Christians often refer to it as "the
will of God." But whatever we call it, we generally settle for nothing less than our version of how life ought to be.

Any searcher for the ideal life only needs to look at the Garden of Eden to see the futility of that pursuit. Adam and Eve lived in paradise—*literally*. Think about it. They had an unspoiled environment, the perfect spouse, a fulfilling occupation, plenty of food, and an easy decision of what to wear each day—nothing! They lived without a care in the world and with no sin to mar their motives. It was an ideal life in every sense of the word.

And yet it wasn't enough. Even paradise had its limitations.

Along with that ideal life, deep within their hearts resided the possibility of discontent. Understand, this possibility wasn't sin—but it represented a necessary *potential* in their relationship with God. Because they *could sin*, it meant their worship of God originated from their wills, not from their reflexes. They *chose* to obey—or not. In other words, their ideal life had nothing to do with what went wrong. In the midst of that ideal life, they chose to sin.

Their circumstances were irrelevant. That's important to remember as we follow God's plan for our lives. Finding God's will doesn't mean finding utopia. Even in the midst of God's will for us, there will be snakes. Temptations will come. Brothers will drop us in pits. Our multicolored coats will get torn off.

Our career won't make life all we want it to be. Neither will a husband, or a wife, or children, or a house, or a church—or any situation. That's the lie of the devil, echoing from Eden. That's the futility of chasing the ideal.

The mantra of today is "Follow your heart." It's the moral lesson of most movies. It's the guiding light of many lives: *Just look within yourself and see who you are and then be that person.* After all, it sounds so right, doesn't it? But following our heart is just another way of following our feelings. As Christians, we usually phrase it in more spiritual terms: "I don't have a peace about this decision," or "I don't sense God's leading here," or "I prayed about it and I feel it's okay to do."

Although our feelings are real, they may not represent reality. And even if what we feel does have some connection to reality, it never reflects *all* of reality. There's always more God sees that we cannot see. We view life from a limited perspective, so we need to resist the assumption that because we feel something strongly, it must be true. True feelings don't equate with truth.

When God the Father spun the earth into orbit millennia ago, he knew we would need a guide to lead us through the deceptions of Satan and the maze of our own emotions.

Obedience is that guide.

If we could see life from God's perspective, we would realize the obedient way is the *best* way. The path of obedience always leads to the life we want because it always follows the big picture God sees. We need to make it a habit to evaluate our feelings through the grid of God's Word. We should always ask ourselves, *What does the Bible say about this decision? What is the obedient way?* And what should we do when there is a contradiction between our heart and the Bible?

We should betray our feelings. We mustn't follow our heart. Remember Jeremiah's question we examined in chapter 9: "The heart is more deceitful than all else and is desperately sick; who can understand it?" (Jer. 17:9).

On the contrary, we should trust in the Lord with all our heart, and never lean on our own understanding (see Prov. 3:5–6).

Even when that means humbling ourselves—like Joseph did.

Even when we have to stand alone to do it—like Joseph did.

Even when it requires facing our fears—like Joseph did.

Joseph understood that obedience was the path to walk, every single time, even when everything seemed to contradict that principle.

Remember that if we follow our heart and allow feelings to guide us, the results can lead us into places that will make us *feel* much, much worse. Think Jacob. Think Reuben. Think Simeon. Think Judah. Think of many people you know.

The ideal life we're searching for is not what we really want—that is, if we could see the big picture like God does. In God's wisdom and because he loves us, he gives us the life we get, not the life we want.

What proved true at one end of the book of Genesis with Adam and Eve also proved true on the other end with Joseph. It's true for us as well. Whether we face a serpent in paradise or a coffin in Egypt, our circumstances should always rank second to our will to obey God. Our challenge is to cling to what God says even when everything within us demands we run the other way.

Although it seldom feels true, obedience is the ideal life we're seeking.

It's just tough to see that sometimes.

When we close one eye and look closely at a marble, the little glass ball seems massive. In fact, the marble is all we see. It dwarfs everything else. But its size is an illusion. A basketball is much bigger. The planet earth is much, much bigger. And God is infinitely bigger than our marble. Our problems are like that.

Life has lots of marbles. When we fixate on our marbles, we can't see the reality that they are small in comparison to God's power. Sure, they're real. Of course they hurt. But our life is more than our problems, just as the world is more than our marbles. Or it can be. We only need to sit up, refocus, and get perspective.

I'll never forget the moment I put on my first eyeglasses at age thirteen. The world came alive! Trees had leaves. Shapes had edges. Colors looked vibrant. These details had been there all the time, of course, but my nearsightedness hid them from me.

Fast-forward thirty-five years to today, and now I have another problem. I can see just fine far away with my contacts in, but not up close. Or I can take out the contacts and see just fine up close, but not far away. It's one perspective or the other. But having worn contact lenses for years, I really don't want to go back to wagging around glasses just to read. Nor do I want bifocals yet. Tough customer, I know.

My optometrist offered me a strange solution: a different prescription for each eye. With one eye I would read, and with the other eye I would see far away.

Huh? At first, this sounded nuts. Wouldn't that make *everything* blurry?

But the doctor explained that in time my brain would "rewire" my vision to where I didn't notice the blur anymore. Everything would get clear. You know what? It works.

This got me thinking of the perspective in our spiritual lives. We tend to have the problem of seeing either what's close or what's far. But we need to learn to see both at the same time.

We need to pay attention to our daily lives, of course—to the things nearby—by growing in essential qualities of spiritual maturity (see 2 Pet. 1:8). At the same time, a balanced perspective requires we keep another eyeball on the things far away—on eternal things. Peter reminds us why: "For he who lacks these qualities is blind or short-sighted, having forgotten his purification from his former sins" (v. 9). The term *shortsighted* literally means *nearsighted*. In fact, from Peter's original Greek word we get the word *myopia*.

Spiritual myopia can blur our lives when we forget our salvation. If we forget about what Jesus did for us—even for a little while—we can't see eternity as clearly. On the other hand, neither can we focus so much on heaven or Bible study that the rafters sag and the roof leaks. We must see today's activities with an eternal perspective in order to keep a balanced view. We need to focus on both perspectives through the lenses of Scripture. As we do, our minds are "rewired" (renewed) and we see both perspectives clearly.

On the day Joseph's brothers dropped him in the pit at Dothan, neither they nor Joseph gave one thought about how that decision would affect eternity. It was all about the here and now. A huge bag of marbles. But in hindsight, both Joseph and his brothers saw God's hand in the events and interpreted them accordingly. Hindsight provided insight. It always can.

Interestingly, Dothan appears in the Bible only twice. The other occasion occurred centuries later, when Elisha and his servant awoke one morning in Dothan to discover the city surrounded by a vast enemy army. The servant saw the large number of chariots and horses and panicked. So Elisha prayed, "O LORD, I pray, open his eyes that he may see" (2 Kings 6:17). Suddenly, the servant saw angelic "horses and chariots of fire all around Elisha." Elisha saw both realms, the natural and the spiritual, and told his servant, "Do not fear, for those who are with us are more than those who are with them" (v. 16). Foresight provided insight. It always can, just like hindsight.

We ought to impose the truths of Elisha's experience at Dothan upon Joseph's earlier experience there. Everything *seemed* to play out against Joseph—the brothers' hatred, the father's favoritism, the chance directions from a stranger, the lushness of the area, the international highway to Egypt, the Ishmaelites who happened by—all these elements revealed God's sovereignty in the goings on. In hindsight, we see God *very* much involved. But at the time of the crisis he seemed *very* much absent. Yet he wasn't. The participants had only one eye open.

In the same way, we can trust that the details of our present struggle serve as vital parts of God's grand plan. With one eye we see our struggles. With the other eye we see by faith that God has purpose for it all. One eye sees the chaos in the world. The other eye sees God working.

We need both eyes, because sometimes it seems God is doing nothing.

My wife, Cathy, planted potatoes in our garden one year, and several days later I walked by and looked. Guess what? Those potatoes hadn't grown an inch. Moreover, after weeks of seeing nothing grow, I could have felt the temptation to doubt if Cathy had planted any potatoes at all—even though I saw her do it.

Jesus used this type of situation to teach us about God's plan in the world:

> The kingdom of God is like a man who casts seed upon the soil; and he goes to bed at night and gets up by day, and the seed sprouts and grows—how, he himself does not know. The soil produces crops by itself; first the blade, then the head, then the mature grain in the head. But when the crop permits, he immediately puts in the sickle, because the harvest has come. (Mark 4:26–29)

When we plant a seed, we participate in a process we can't comprehend. The process happens "by itself"—a phrase that comes from the Greek term *automate*. Just as God programmed a seed to sprout by itself, and we have no clue how, so he does the same with his kingdom plan in the world.

The process as Jesus described it—"first the blade, then the head, then the mature grain"—suggests a progression of steps, none of which we can hurry, skip, or delay. We can only wait.

Then Jesus spoke about a tiny mustard seed that, "though it is smaller than all the seeds that are upon the soil, yet when it is sown, it grows up and becomes larger than all the garden plants" (vv. 31–32). God's plan is progressing in spite of its seeming insignificance now. God's kingdom work seems like a mustard seed. Small, insignificant, and ineffective. But God works in ways that human eyes can't see. He is sowing seeds that await a certain harvest. Jesus's parables reveal that what seems hidden today will one day become visible to all.

In an age of instant everything, Jesus urges us to use both eyeballs. We need a persistent faith that looks toward a certain and overwhelming outcome. God's sovereign plan is progressing in spite of what we see or don't see—or don't understand.

Last spring Cathy and I walked down a country road near our home and saw the spring leaves popping from the trees. Literally a week earlier the branches had nothing. One week! It got me thinking. All the potential for the trees to leaf lay hidden, dormant all winter, until something inside the trees awakened them from their slumber and they pushed out to life.

Life was there all the time, hiding behind death, until something cued it to resurrect.

If this is how the earth responds to the stimulus of the seasons, how much more potential lies dormant in creation, awaiting the moment God removes the effects of fallen humanity from our planet? God told Adam, "Cursed is the ground because of you" (Gen. 3:17). Adam's name means *man*, and it corresponds to the term *adamah*, referring to the "ground" from which God formed him. Accordingly, when Adam sinned, God cursed the ground to which Adam would return when he died.

But when God removes the curse of sin from humanity, the creation will also enjoy a resurrection of sorts.

> For the anxious longing of the creation waits eagerly for the revealing of the sons of God. For the creation was subjected to futility, not willingly, but because of Him who subjected it, in hope that the creation itself also will be set free from its slavery to corruption into the freedom of the glory of the children of God. For we know that the whole creation groans and suffers the pains of childbirth together until now. And not only this, but also we . . . groan within ourselves, waiting eagerly for our adoption as sons, the redemption of our body. (Rom. 8:19–23)

Any woman who has experienced childbirth can relate to the Bible's metaphor. Any helpless man who has witnessed childbirth (as I have, twice) can relate in a small way. (I think kidney stones count too, by the way. But let's stick with childbirth. It well illustrates our struggle.)

Life hurts.

We would all love to have an emotional epidural to take the edge off life's contractions. But God doesn't give us a way to avoid the hurt. Instead, he tells us *what to think* so we can push through the struggle.

Pain is universal in that the whole creation groans and suffers. That includes you and me. That includes the person on the far side of the globe. That includes the person you see whom you think has it all together. It includes millionaires and billionaires. It includes your pastor and his family. It even included Jesus.

Everybody hurts.

And placing our faith in Jesus Christ changes nothing with regard to our feeling pain in life. The Christian life even brings new kinds of struggles.

Our present sufferings are huge. Like giving birth. Most times, they distract and dominate our lives with pain so intense we can't imagine it will ever quit. The Bible never diminishes the reality of our struggles. Not once. Instead, the Scriptures challenge us to put them in perspective. To see with both eyes.

Like it is in childbirth, our pain in life is intense. But it is also *temporary*. For a new mother, the pain is hard up to a point— until the baby comes. Likewise, the severe pain of this life, for the Christian, concludes when *the Person* comes. Paul wrote, "For I consider that the sufferings of this present time are not worthy to be compared with the glory that is to be revealed to us" (v. 18). That means the worst pain we have ever felt cannot compare with the joy that awaits us in glory. Try to imagine the truth of that for a moment.

But when we've waited and waited and waited on God for years, honestly, after a while, our hearts can get discouraged and despairing. We have huge, cavernous gaps in life where we wonder if God has found something better to do than to help us out. As Solomon wrote, "Hope deferred makes the heart sick" (Prov. 13:12). We need affirmation of our hope.

I love that God gave Joseph encouragement all along the way. The Lord blessed Joseph's work wherever he served. His correct interpretations of others' dreams gave him confidence God had not forgotten him.

In the same way, I have discovered that if we keep both eyes open, and stay ready for God's encouragement, we will see it. It may come through a preacher's message. It might come through a verse we read in our quiet times. A friend can boost us on God's behalf. So can a book. So can a song. Perhaps we can glean encouragement from God's faithfulness as we see the seasons change, right on schedule, every single year.

When we buy a car, we begin to see that same car everywhere. Did our make and model suddenly appear on the streets? No, we just became *more aware* of its presence. If we determine to keep both eyes open, if we don't fixate on our marbles, we begin to see the Lord's encouragement that helps us press on.

God helps us keep waiting for a certain hope. I love Eugene Peterson's paraphrase of Romans 8:24: "Waiting does not diminish us, any more than waiting diminishes a pregnant mother. We are enlarged in the waiting" (Message).

Our hope in God's kingdom certainly is deferred, but it is also certain. Read David's words slowly, thoughtfully, and aloud if you can:

> I would have despaired unless I had believed that I would see the goodness of the LORD in the land of the living. Wait for the LORD; be strong and let your heart take courage; yes, wait for the LORD. (Ps. 27:13–14)

This is a person with both eyes open—one near and one far. This is who we must become.

Too often we see ourselves waiting on God for solutions that can happen only in this life. If Joseph's final words teach us anything, they reveal that the majority of the hopes we're waiting on God to fulfill don't happen until our resurrection. (Stop. Read that again.) This comes as a tough pill to choke down. But we must fight the gag reflex of our fallen nature and swallow hard. The life of faith is one that looks beyond this life to the reality of the next.

I waited all my life for God to give my mother sobriety and for her to devote her life to serving him. What's more, in my Bible, I have my mother's name inked in beside Luke 18:1–7, which I often prayed for her by name: "Will not God bring about justice for His elect who cry to Him day and night, and will He delay long over them?" (v. 7). And what happened? Mom died intoxicated. What I prayed for her for years never happened in this life.

But this life is not all of life. It's only the beginning.

Oh, death makes it *look* like this is all there is. Death has such a brutal finality to it, doesn't it? It looks terribly convincing. It can kill dreams.

I think about Jacob when I think about the death of dreams. Jacob worked for fourteen years to earn the right to marry Rachel. Then they struggled for years to have children, until finally she gave birth to Joseph. Then Jacob labored for six years to build up their flocks. But what happened? Not long after they returned to Canaan—after twenty-plus years of dreaming about the future, and at the beginning of what Jacob would have considered the reward of his hard work—Rachel died giving birth to Benjamin.

He had worked all his life and now there was *no* chance of his dreams coming true. He had just buried them.

No wonder Jacob clung to Joseph and Benjamin like he did. God had to take them away and give them back before Jacob would confess at the end of his life, "For Your salvation I wait, O LORD" (Gen. 49:18).

Our ideal life isn't found here. If this life is all there is to living, then, as the apostle Paul wrote, "We are of all men most to be pitied" (1 Cor. 15:19). Instead, we must keep eternity in view. It takes both eyeballs.

A godly mind looks at the hard facts of today, but it also looks beyond them to future facts just as true. That's faith. Faith focuses on eternal facts, not just the fast facts. Faith takes the long view and makes decisions based on long-term results. If we have no moral solution to our desires, obedience demands we wait on God for the fulfillment—or for the maturity—of those desires. It's possible, after all, that what we want really stems from selfishness.

This life spans less than a blip on eternity's chronometer. So why do we demand God give us all his promises in this blip? We need to view our waiting in the difficulties of our daily living as opportunities to demonstrate faith in a future promised by our sovereign God.

Even death—the painful blow that seems so utterly final—merely represents our greatest opportunity to demonstrate our faith in God's sovereignty.

Joseph's final words point beyond his life to a future he confidently believed would come: "God will surely take care of you, and you shall carry my bones up from here" (Gen. 50:25). We could literally translate his first phrase this way: "God will surely visit you." Joseph was so sure that he said the phrase *twice* on his deathbed (see vv. 24–25). The original term for *visit* has more meaning than a simple social call. It speaks of God's power coming for blessing or judgment. Joseph's words point to the exodus, of course, but "visit" looks beyond that event—and even beyond the Old Testament itself—to a final redemption on a cosmic scale.

The promise of God's visitation finds no reoccurrence in Scripture until the priest Zacharias and his wife, Elizabeth, celebrate the birth of their son, John the Baptist—the forerunner of Jesus Christ. Amazingly, the names of Zacharias and Elizabeth together mean "God remembers his promise." Zacharias expressed it this way:

> Blessed be the Lord God of Israel, for *He has visited* us and accomplished redemption for His people . . . to remember His holy covenant, the oath which He swore to Abraham our father. (Luke 1:68, 72–73, emphasis added)

God visited earth when Jesus came and offered salvation—though many rejected him (see 19:44). But he is coming again to get us—and then to rule the world.

I love the succinct way Paul summarized the lives of the Thessalonian believers, whose purpose was "to serve a living and true God, and to wait for His Son from heaven" (1 Thess. 1:9–10). In a nutshell, that's our calling.

We serve and we wait.

While we serve and wait, Jesus has gone to prepare a place for us. The apostle John wrote of Jesus's promise to come again and take us who believe in him to be with him (see John 14:2–3). John also wrote what our lives will be like in eternity: "His bond-servants will serve Him; they will see His face, and His name will be on their foreheads" (Rev. 22:3–4).

God's name on our foreheads? What makes that significant?

Have you ever found out what your name means? My wife's name, Cathy, means "pure." My brother's name, Matthew, means "gift of God." You know what my name, Wayne, means?

"Wagon maker."

Yep. No joke. (Hey, at least I'm not walking.)

For years, I figured my grandfather and I were the only two humans in the world named "Wayne Stiles." Then one day a quick search on the web proved me wrong. There are a lot of us! The most well-known among my namesakes designed beautiful golf courses. Nice. Why do we Google our names? Our names represent *us*—and we want our names well represented. (By the way, remember that other people with your name will Google you. Make them proud.)

Something more significant than a name given at birth occurs when God changes a name. Abraham, Sarah, Israel, and Peter are a few of the new names the Lord gave to people. When God changes a *name*, he changes a *person*. It indicates something new has happened or will happen to that person—a new relationship, a new character quality, or a new phase of life. A name represents the person.

That's what makes God's name on our foreheads so significant. We're *his*.

> I will give him . . . a new name written on the stone which no one knows but he who receives it. . . . I will write on him the name of My God, and the name of the city of My God, the new Jerusalem, which comes down out of heaven from My God, and My new name. (Rev. 2:17; 3:12)

Just look at all those names Jesus will bestow on us! They all represent the magnificent changes the Lord will make possible by his grace.

I can still hear it: "We have gathered here today to remember the life of Wayne Stiles."

I'll never forget those words at my grandfather's funeral. As I stood there, it hit me: *You know, one day someone will say those words again.* I hope when that time comes, somebody will stand and share with those who have gathered that I am in heaven because of the grace of my Lord Jesus Christ—who died for my sins and rose again—and not because of the life that I lived.

Someday, someone will stand and speak for all of us.

The road of our lives leads to death, but it never ends there. Our bodies rest in a grave, but our souls bounce and never slow down. Angels usher us into the presence of God until the day our spirits reunite with our bodies, resurrected to meet Jesus in the air—never to die again (see Luke 16:22; 1 Cor. 15:51–55; 1 Thess. 4:16).

When I imagine heaven, I picture the bright streets of gold and the pearly gates and the awesome beauty of an unspoiled place. But these things are only the stage upon which the joy of eternity occurs.

The true blessing of heaven will be its occupants. That's the joy of heaven! I look forward to seeing my grandparents, Wayne, Doris, Jack, and Ella. I want to see other family and friends who have gone before me, such as Charles, Sherry, Lori, and others I have lost over the years. I also want to see my mother—especially the joy on her face as she beholds her Savior, the man she has already adored for more than eleven years now. I look forward to seeing the saints of old, such as Abraham, Ruth, Paul, and Peter. And I really look forward to seeing Joseph.

But most of all, of course—*far* above everyone else—I long to look into the face of my Savior. I want to look in his eyes, embrace him, and thank him endlessly. Then I want to tell him my best joke and make him laugh.

Perhaps you have discovered, as I have, that heaven seems far more real the more people we know who have gone there ahead of us. Our loved ones who have died are like the leaves inside branches waiting for the spring. Life is still there, hiding behind death, until something cues it to resurrect. Timothy Keller reminds us, "Resurrection is not just consolation—it is restoration. We get it all back—the love, the loved ones, the goods, the beauties of this life—but in new, unimaginable degrees of glory and joy and strength."[1]

Have you buried a dream when you buried a loved one? Remember, this life, as real as it is, represents only a slice of reality—just a fraction of our total existence. Heaven is a lot longer than the dash on our tombstones. Our death is but a doorway to God's broad expanse of eternity. His promises extend beyond the grave.

This life is only the foyer to forever. God made us for eternity.

Every person in the Scriptures who had the occasion to catch a glimpse of the Almighty hit the dirt in a coil of shame and terror. But one day we will gaze full into his eyes and marvel at his holiness without fear of punishment, because Jesus took that penalty when he died for us. We will see God not in parables, not in metaphors, not in the enigma of Scripture, not in the evidence of creation, and not in a mirror dimly. But face-to-face.

With our own eyes, we will see the face of God. Imagine that for a moment, if you can.

You . . . seeing the face of God.

It's going to happen, and it's more certain than your next breath.

God recorded Joseph's life for us as more than a good read. Charles Hodge wrote, "What is true of the history of Joseph, is true of all of history."[2] It isn't just a great story. It's *your* story—and it's mine.

The Bible doesn't tell us everything. It doesn't need to. It tells us all we need to know in order to live a life of faith. The rest, we wait for.

Whatever it is you're waiting on God for, remember that the fulfillment of all your longings is ultimately found in Jesus. You may have been waiting on God for a long time already. Don't allow

God's delay to distract you from faithfulness. "The Lord is not slow about His promise, as some count slowness," Peter reminds us (2 Pet. 3:9). God's patience has purpose.

God's delay doesn't represent his apathy. He has something special planned.

Even if you wait your whole life, you have God's promise that Christ will make all things right for you—and in you—when he comes for you. I love the words of Adoniram Judson: "When Christ calls me home, I shall go with the gladness of a boy bounding away from his school."[3]

Can't you just picture that? Carefree—and *free*.

Finally, *really free*.

The last words from Joseph's lips express so well our own hope. We yearn for the finale of God's visitation. We long for our resurrection—for the day when the Lion of Judah, the Lord Jesus Christ, comes to get us.

The hope Joseph expressed in his final words we find magnificently affirmed in the promise of Jesus in his final words in the Bible:

"Yes, I am coming quickly." Amen. Come, Lord Jesus. (Rev. 22:20)

That, my friends, is what we're waiting for.

ACKNOWLEDGMENTS

Most musicians have had the question asked of them, "How long did you have to practice for your concert?" The answer sounds humorous, but it's true.

"All my life."

That's how I feel about this book. These pages represent lessons I've learned over the course of my lifetime—as well as principles that will take me a lifetime to learn. All of these chapters contain content I have scraped from the pages of my journals and memories.

At the same time, a book, like any other worthy work, always represents the dedication and influence of many people—not just its author. Here are a few.

I'm grateful to Chip MacGregor for believing in my writing enough to represent me. If he ever fails as a literary agent, he has a career waiting as a stand-up comic. (No joke.)

Thanks to the outstanding team at Baker Books: Rebekah Guzman, Lindsey Spoolstra, Lauren Carlson, Heather Brewer, Mark Rice, and Dave Lewis. Their excellence in communication, care, and attention to detail has made this project a joy from start to finish.

The longer I serve in ministry, the more grateful and indebted I become for the outstanding theological training I received from Dallas Theological Seminary under the capable leadership of three presidents: Dr. Donald Campbell, Dr. Charles R. Swindoll, and Dr. Mark Bailey. That fine institution and its outstanding faculty have helped me understand and teach the Bible with accuracy and confidence—and most importantly, they have helped me be more like the Bible's central character, Jesus.

Thanks to Dr. Sandi Glahn for her ceaseless support of my writing and to *Kindred Spirit* magazine for allowing me to adapt my daughter-tossing article that appears in chapter 7.

Thanks to my colleagues at Insight for Living Ministries, particularly Bill Gemaehlich, Todd Turner, and Tom Hayes for their friendship, leadership, and devotion to our staff. I'm grateful to Cynthia Swindoll for allowing me to take a few vacation days to devote myself entirely to completing this book. Thanks to Jim Craft, Paula McCoy, Megan Meckstroth, Katy Robertson, Malia Rodriguez, Sharifa Stevens, LeeAnna Swartz, and Colleen Swindoll Thompson—my fine co-workers in the creative ministries department, of whom I admire their commitment to communicating God's Word in words that change lives. I also appreciate the many evenings of Bible study and friendship Mark and Deedee Snyder have devoted to Cathy and me.

Thanks so much to Margaret Gulliford for her outstanding work on the map on page 10. I appreciate her willingness and enthusiasm to help me create it for this book.

Thanks to Dr. Stan and Max Toussaint for their years of devotion in our Adult Fellowship Marathon class and for forty-seven fruitful years of teaching at Dallas Theological Seminary.

Thanks to Allen P. Ross for his excellent book *Creation and Blessing*. I culled many observations and ideas from this fine author and volume.

Thanks to Fernando Ortega, Hayley Westenra, U2, John Williams, Marc Shaiman, Harry Gregson-Williams, and Ennio

Morricone for their musical inspiration that undergirded many words in this book.

Thanks to the friendly baristas of Starbucks at Preston and Stonebrook in Plano, Texas: Lauren, Stella, Dana, David, Bekah, Katie, Anna, Brenna, Kristi, and Molly (and all the newbies). I'm grateful for their hospitality, for their tasty Pike Place roast, and for giving me a corner to scribble in most weekday mornings.

Thanks to Matt and Catherine Stephens for teaching Emma and Avery in words and in actions to know the Lord Jesus. I love knowing that Matt, my brother in life, is my brother in Christ. I have dedicated this book to him.

Thanks to James and Courtney Webber for the privilege of officiating at their wedding. I appreciate them for the courage and compassion they displayed by wanting the love of Christ shared with all their friends and family. I love knowing that Courtney, my sister in life, is my sister in Christ. I have dedicated this book to her.

Thanks to Sarah and Kate, the two godliest young women I know. I respect and admire them more every year for their commitment to the gospel, for pursuing lives for God's glory, and for striving to love Jesus more than any earthly thing. "I have no greater joy than this, to hear of my children walking in the truth" (3 John 4).

Thanks to Cathy, my wife of twenty-six years, who has an undying passion for God and his Word, a love of serving, a wonderful way with children and the aged, an authentic compassion for the lost, and a genuine desire to become more like our Savior.

Finally, a standing ovation goes to my favorite person in the Bible, Joseph. So much of his life truly deserves esteem. I think I appreciate most of all that at the end of his incredible life, he pointed to God and not to himself.

I want my life to do the same.

Our citizenship is in heaven, from which also we eagerly wait for a Savior, the Lord Jesus Christ. (Phil. 3:20)

NOTE TO THE READER

Dear Friend,

Before you ever picked up this book, I prayed for you. I prayed that Joseph's life would encourage you to wait on God as he reveals his wise plan for your life.

My hope is that our time together in the magnificent life of Joseph has reignited your confidence in our sovereign God's control and refreshed your hope in the certainty of heaven.

I would love to hear from you.

Feel free to connect with me on my blog and subscribe to get my regular email devotionals.

May the Lord bless you as you wait on him,

www.waynestiles.com

NOTES

Chapter 1 Living in the Gaps with God

1. Blaise Pascal, *Pensées* (Stilwell: KS, Digireads.com, 2005), 57.

Chapter 3 Satisfaction on Hold

1. John Owen, *The Mortification of Sin* (Edinburgh: Banner of Truth, 2004), 55.

Chapter 4 Going Backward, Moving Forward

1. David Dorsey, *The Literary Structure of the Old Testament* (Grand Rapids: Baker, 1999), 16.

2. Thomas Aquinas, *A Shorter Summa: The Most Essential Philosophical Passages of Saint Thomas Aquinas' Summa Theologica*, ed. Peter Kreeft (San Francisco: Ignatius Press, 1993), 144.

3. Augustine, *Confessions*, 2nd ed., trans. F. J. Sheed, ed. Michael P. Foley (Indianapolis, IN: Hackett, 2006), 3.

Chapter 6 The Opportunity of Obscurity

1. As quoted in Ernest Becker, *The Birth and Death of Meaning: An Interdisciplinary Perspective on the Problem of Man* (New York: The Free Press, 1971), 123.

Chapter 7 The Surprising Place Where Waiting Begins

1. This story adapted from Wayne Stiles, "In Good Hands," *Kindred Spirit* 30, no. 3, September 5, 2006, http://www.dts.edu/read/in-good-hands-wayne-stiles/.

2. Derek Kidner, *Proverbs: An Introduction and Commentary* (Wheaton: Tyndale, 2009), 35.

3. Joe Dallas, *The Game Plan* (Nashville: Thomas Nelson), Kindle ed., loc. 686–91.

Chapter 8 A Long Resolution

1. Dorsey, *Literary Structure*, 60.
2. John Flavel, *Navigation Spiritualized: Or, A New Compass for Seamen* (New-Town: J. Bennett, 1822), 121.

Chapter 9 When Forgiving Someone Is Hard

1. Dustin Shramek, "Waiting for the Morning during the Long Night of Weeping," in *Suffering and the Sovereignty of God*, ed. John Piper and Justin Taylor (Wheaton: Crossway, 2006), 175.
2. Mary DeMuth, *The Wall around Your Heart: How Jesus Heals You When Others Hurt You* (Nashville: Thomas Nelson, 2013), 116.

Chapter 10 The Hope of Dying with Unfulfilled Dreams

1. Jennifer Rothschild, *God Is Just Not Fair: Finding Hope When Life Doesn't Make Sense* (Grand Rapids: Zondervan, 2014), Kindle ed., loc. 1158.
2. Doug Petrovich, "Joseph in Egypt: Part I," *Associates for Biblical Research*, February 18, 2014, http://www.biblearchaeology.org/post/2010/02/18/Joseph-in-Egypt-Part-I.aspx.

Chapter 11 What You've Been Waiting For

1. Timothy Keller, *Walking with God through Pain and Suffering* (New York: Dutton, 2013), 59.
2. Charles Hodge, *Systematic Theology*, vol. 1 (Grand Rapids: Eerdmans, 1986), 544.
3. Mrs. H. C. Conant, *The Earnest Man: A Sketch of the Character and Labors of Adoniram Judson* (Boston: Philipps, Samson and Company, 1856), 495.

Connect with Wayne Stiles

on his blog: www.waynestiles.com

Using his love for the Bible and its lands, Wayne Stiles provides

engaging devotionals and resources to encourage your relationship

with God. When you subscribe to Wayne's blog, he will send you

a free ebook and fresh content each time he posts. Best of all,

you will discover the wonderful transformation that occurs

by connecting the Bible and its lands to your life.

Walking in His Footsteps
Can Change Your Life

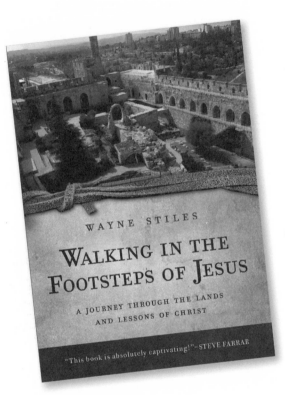

Imagine following Jesus along the road, listening in on his conversations, and gleaning personal insights he taught in the holy places he traveled. This book will take you there.

Take a Devotional Journey
Through the Lands of the Bible

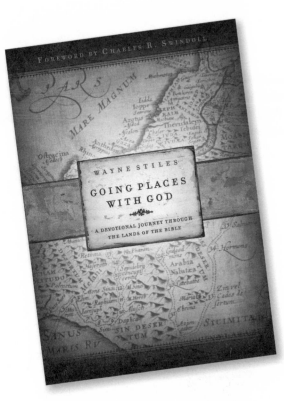

After going places with God, you'll never be the same . . .

These ninety devotional readings, each based on a specific
place in the lands of the Bible, invite you to embark
on your own spiritual journey with God.